INNOVATIVE
INSURANCE

INNOVATIVE INSURANCE

HOW TO LOWER YOUR RISK AND BUILD A MORE SUCCESSFUL
REAL ESTATE INVESTMENT BUSINESS

SHAWN WOEDL

Advantage | Books

Published by Advantage, Charleston, South Carolina.
Member of Advantage Media.

ADVANTAGE is a registered trademark, and the Advantage colophon is a trademark of Advantage Media Group, Inc.

Printed in the United States of America.

10 9 8 7 6 5 4 3 2 1

ISBN: 978-1-64225-606-2 (Paperback)
ISBN: 978-1-64225-605-5 (eBook)

LCCN: 2023902604

Cover design by Wesley Strickland.
Layout design by Matthew Morse.

This publication is designed to provide accurate and authoritative information in regard to the subject matter covered. It is sold with the understanding that the publisher is not engaged in rendering legal, accounting, or other professional services. If legal advice or other expert assistance is required, the services of a competent professional person should be sought.

Advantage Media helps busy entrepreneurs, CEOs, and leaders write and publish a book to grow their business and become the authority in their field. Advantage authors comprise an exclusive community of industry professionals, idea-makers, and thought leaders. Do you have a book idea or manuscript for consideration? We would love to hear from you at **AdvantageMedia.com**.

To my wife and kids, who have sacrificed so much more than I have these last fifteen-plus years. Thank you for your patience, support, and understanding. I love you.

Being relentless means never being satisfied. It means creating new goals every time you reach your personal best. If you're good, it means you don't stop until you're great. If you're great, it means you fight until you're unstoppable. It means becoming a Cleaner.

TIM S. GROVER, *RELENTLESS: FROM GOOD TO GREAT TO UNSTOPPABLE*

CONTENTS

ACKNOWLEDGMENTS

Tim Norris—thank you for everything. I have no words.

Chelsea Ames, Heidi Scott, Jacqui Price, Jason Jones, and Julie Prewitt—your contributions to this book are invaluable. Thank you for sticking with me through this.

My "ride or die" crew: Anthony Eardley, Nick Thompson, Terrence Duffy, and Thad Crane. Since day one and until the end. Thank you.

Beets—who challenges me to be better every day. Even when I'm being difficult.

DISCLAIMER

The information in this book is intended to provide readers with general information, suggestions, and recommendations on matters that they might find to be of interest in the field of real estate investment insurance. This information is not intended to constitute legal advice and should not replace or serve as a substitute for any professional or legal recommendations, consultation, or service. Readers should make decisions that best suit their specific business model, investment goals, and appetite for risk, and they should consult with a professional advisor concerning insurance, finance, and any other related matter before making those decisions.

INTRODUCTION

Insurance.

I can see your eyes glazing over now. Who wants to talk about insurance when there are so many other interesting things we could talk about? Like, what's in Area 51, anyway? Or is Bigfoot just one creature or a whole species? Or what does my Chinese Zodiac sign really mean?

But you must have some interest in the topic, or you wouldn't be reading this right now.

Maybe you are an up-and-coming new broker, eager to learn the ropes. Maybe you are a seasoned investor who is sick of getting burned. Maybe you are a fresh-faced first-time flipper just trying to make a go of this exciting new project.

Regardless of why you are here, this book will help you navigate the land mines of the insurance landscape and minimize your risk. Even if you take away only one or two hints, you'll be miles ahead of your colleagues, because this book gives you the insider track. You'll come away knowing the difference between one policy and another and be able to interpret the terminology that could harm you.

Why am I here? And why should you listen to me?

Well, you should listen because I've spent the last fifteen years of my career helping investors like you make the right decisions for their businesses. My name is Shawn Woedl, and I am the CEO and president of National Real Estate Insurance Group (NREIG). We are an independent insurance agency that specializes in the specific and often underserved needs of real estate investors. NREIG started in 2008 in a basement office in Cincinnati, Ohio, where we initially built the business by speaking at different Real Estate Investment Association (REIA) groups across Ohio. They didn't have an insurance presence there, and we discovered that nobody was around to educate their base on insuring their properties the right way. The light bulb kind of went on, and now we've grown to over 140,000 locations across all fifty states with over 20,000 investors enrolled in our programs. An overwhelming majority of those clients are fantastic. They are people who understand that we're just out to help them. We're working as an advocate on their behalf to find the coverage package that's best for them to protect their professional livelihoods.

Throughout my years of experience as an insurance broker, I have seen a kind of black eye on this industry in the way that insurance salesmen are perceived in our culture. I am aware that we brought some of it on ourselves. But that's no excuse to allow things to go on unchecked.

I'm not naive enough to think I can change the world, or even this industry, but I can control what the people who work for me offer to our clients, partners, and the industry. I can control the quality of our products and whom I partner with. I can clean up the space where I sit. I want to bring along the next generation of agents and teach them what I've learned, and, when I am gone, I hope they will approach the industry the same way I do.

I want to leave the industry better than I found it. Part of achieving that goal includes helping to strengthen the consumers we serve. When you know what questions to ask and how to find the best products for your needs, that keeps us on our toes. I want to be challenged, because I firmly believe in the saying by Rear Admiral Grace Hopper: "The most dangerous phrase in the language is, 'We have always done it this way.'"[1]

My hope is that the information I share in this book will benefit your business in a tangible way. This could look like you feeling empowered to confront your agent and challenging him or her to find better alternatives for you. I hope to protect you from claim scenarios that you couldn't see coming. And I hope to help you look more critically at yourself and look for ways you may be open to unnecessary and preventable risk. Then you can use that knowledge to obtain the support and service you need and deserve from your agent. For me, that's a win.

---

1   "Dr. Grace Hopper," DDSN Interactive, last modified September 4, 2020, https:// ddsn.com/blog/digital-design-service-technology-quotes/dr-grace-hopper.html.

CHAPTER 1

WHY DO WE EVEN HAVE INSURANCE, ANYWAY?

What's the first thing that comes to mind when you hear the word "insurance"? Is it a big, bad, scary word that belongs in hushed conversations in dark rooms? Or does it describe a protective covering and resource to provide safety and security after a loss or in the midst of sudden adversity?

Regardless of whether you shudder or laugh or your eyes glaze over when you think about insurance, it is a necessity in the world we live in and is particularly crucial if you are a real estate investor. An investor I knew recently bought a rental property in a location that was far from his home, so he hired a property management group to manage it for him. The property management firm had been holding the insurance policy previously, but the new owner wanted to take control of the insurance himself. So they notified the insurance broker that they were canceling their policy to allow him to take over. The owner received several emails from the broker instructing him on what to do to insure his new property, but, like everyone, he opened the messages and just glanced over them. He figured he'd get around to taking care of it all soon.

Since this is a book about insurance, you can probably guess what happened next. A fire destroyed the property right in that in-between time when it was uninsured. Frantic and begging for help, the owner called the insurance broker. The broker had documented receipt of the emails, so he had every legal right to tell the owner to go pound sand. But he didn't.

The property was a total loss, and there was no way any insurance company was going to restore it, but since it had been insured consistently for a long time previous to this loss, the broker was able to negotiate a settlement with the carrier to help the owner demo the wreckage and clean it up.

I know this is a rare story, but it is one that proves that the insurance industry still has a heart, despite what most people think. I don't recommend taking a chance like this—*ever*. The resolution that came from this example, though true, rarely ends like this for the investor.

Insurance brokers have hearts. And we also have spines.

We've all heard stories of people running insurance scams, like the story from Oneonta, New York. On December 17, 2008, the *Daily Star* newspaper published the story of a bizarre fire that destroyed a home and car. The homeowner explained to investigators that he had been cooking steak on the stove in four different pans. He claimed all four pans caught fire, so he threw a dishrag over them to put the fire out. When that dishrag caught fire (shocking, I know), he claimed he had decided to throw one of the pans out the front door, where it "accidentally" landed on the back seat of his convertible. He said the car immediately caught fire. (Seriously?)

Rather than try to put out the car fire, he ran back inside to grab another pan to throw out. He claimed that he was so flustered that he tripped over a box on the way out and dropped the flaming pan on his leather couch, which (gasp) also went up in flames.

If all of this wasn't suspicious enough, it conveniently turned out he was packing up to move across the country.

While the story reads like a B-movie script, the implications are obvious. Rather than go to the bother of selling his home like everyone else, he came up with this bumbling plan to try to cash in on his homeowner's policy and auto insurance. The insurance companies were not going to be taken advantage of. He was taken to court and ended up pleading guilty to attempted fraud for both his homeowner's and auto policies and was sentenced to five years' probation and over $37,000 in fines and restitution.

INSURANCE IS A TRANSFER OF RISK.

According to the FBI, insurance fraud like this is estimated to cost insurers in the United States more than $40 billion every year, and by some estimates one in thirty insurance claims is fraudulent to some degree, with fire being the largest number of cases.[2] The problem with fire is that arson is highly problematic to prove, so insurance companies often have no choice but to pay and then recoup their costs by raising rates. This drives premiums up by about $400–$700 annually for the average American family.[3]

What a mess. If I were going to sum up the wisdom I have gained in my career as an insurance broker in one sentence, it would be this: insurance is a transfer of risk.

---

2   FBI, "Reports and Publications: Insurance Fraud," fbi.gov, accessed December 15, 2022, https://www.fbi.gov/stats-services/publications/insurance-fraud.

3   Ibid.

Insurance companies are trying to minimize risk, just like you are. And for investors, there is plenty of risk to account for.

Why Do We Even Have Insurance?

Every new development in human history brought a new opportunity for something to go wrong. Discover fire? Now you can get hurt in a manner not previously possible. Invent the wheel? Now you risk damage if you lose control of said new wheels. Domesticate animals? Now you have a risk of injury from bites, scratches, or worse that you didn't have before. What did early man do when they lost everything because of weather or enemies? They had to start over from scratch every time.

Eventually somebody decided there had to be a better way. Disaster and misfortune are good teachers, and humans tend to want to solve problems before they happen. The practice of protecting one's property and life from loss can be found on every continent throughout history with considerations for nearly every conceivable asset, but it took a long time to get here. As far as we know, the first instances of insurance practices were tied to trade, starting as far back as 3000 BC in China. Merchants practiced risk diversification by dividing their wares between multiple ships as they traveled through dangerous waters. Obviously complete loss prevention wasn't always possible, so they did what they could to limit the impact. As civilization expanded and progressed, societies began to come up with new and more relevant ways to protect life and assets.

The Code of Hammurabi, which is the longest ancient legal text ever found, includes a very basic insurance code. It was written in Babylon in 1750 BC and has language in it that was meant to protect boats and cargo from total loss if they sank or got robbed. As an interesting side note, the Code of Hammurabi used money as the basis for every transaction, unlike other ancient Mesopotamian forms of insurance, where sea traders and caravan operators would put up premiums including everything they owned, along with their own families. If goods were lost, they risked being enslaved to pay back the debt.

Insurance was centered on seafaring for centuries after that and settled in a London coffee shop called Edward Lloyd's. By 1866 this small coffee shop had become the center of all maritime insurance policies and was known as Lloyd's of London, still one of the world's leading insurance providers. Lloyd's has significantly expanded since then, now offering a staggering range of policies to cover every conceivable type of risk. Speaking specifically for our program, Lloyd's provides offerings for property coverage, flood coverage, earth movement, tenant protector plans, and liability. But outside the real estate space, they do all kinds of other things too.

From bedbugs to chickens to cold feet at a wedding, you can find an insurance policy that will cover anything that matters to you. And people do. Ever since the 1940s, when film star Betty Grable insured her legs for a million dollars each (with Lloyd's of London, of course), people have been insuring all kinds of crazy things.

Not to be outdone, supermodel Heidi Klum doubled Grable for a total of $4 million for her famous legs. And it has just spiraled from there. Dolly Parton's bosom is covered, as is Tom Jones's chest hair. Keith Richards insured just his middle finger for $1.6 million, and David Beckham insured both his legs and face for $195 million to safeguard both his soccer and modeling careers.

Most of these celebrities have never had to cash in on those policies, but the story is different with Willis McGahee, running back for the University of Miami. Before the Fiesta Bowl game against

Ohio State in 2003, he took out an insurance policy on himself in case he got hurt. He was concerned an injury would damage his draft pick and, sure enough, he broke his leg in that game. His insurance policy paid out millions because his broken leg damaged his future prospects as a top NFL draft pick. It took him two years to rehab, so he was glad to have thought ahead to get that policy. Now it's more common to see a lot of pro and college athletes doing this.

My son is a huge fan of professional wrestling. The people who compete in professional wrestling are always doing crazy stuff that is inherently risky. Can you imagine trying to get health coverage with the kinds of risks they take on every time they get in the ring? With a profession like that, you're going to get hurt, and there are going to be surgeries. Who's going to pay for those surgeries? Thankfully there are supplemental insurance policies for that. No surprise that it's Lloyd's again that offers that sort of thing.

This practice is not just reserved for celebrities or professional athletes. Hayleigh Curtis, a chocolatier with Cadbury, insured her taste buds, and Dutch winemaker Ilja Gort insured his sense of smell. You can even find a policy that protects you in case of alien abduction. (Really! Lloyd's of London is rumored to be carrying more than twenty thousand alien abduction policies at any given time and has even paid out on a few.)

Aliens aside, what does any of this have to do with us? Insurance gives us the peace of mind that we can be made whole if we lose something we value or we need. I have joked with my team that if I couldn't talk, I would be out of business, so I should take a policy out on my own voice!

What Does This Mean for Real Estate Investors?

As a real estate investor, you require a very different approach to insurance to protect your assets. Imagine you just closed on an investment property and have keys in hand. Now what?

Whether you are going to flip it, rent it, renovate it, or do something else, you are immediately at risk. In the amount of time that it takes you to travel from the closing table to that new property, any number of things can go wrong. A fire occurs in the United States every twenty-three seconds. A burglar breaks into another property just as often. Water damage from broken pipes or gas leaks can happen, and nobody will notice until it's too late.

It's enough to make a person want to hand the keys back and find a different way to invest their money. But the benefits of property investment far outweigh the risks if you know what to do. And that's why you do it.

So how do you know the right policies for your specific situation? How do you keep from spending too much on insurance you'll never need? If you search the term "investment property insurance," you will find yourself wading through terms like *agreed value*, *special form policy*, *valued policy law*, *loss settlement methods*, and *subrogation*.

The words "umbrella," "history," and "coverage" take on new meaning in this corner of the insurance world, and most real estate investors are so focused on the goal of the investment that they don't have the time or inclination to learn the nuances. There are certainly good, better, and best ways to protect yourself from risk, but if you simply

> THE BENEFITS OF PROPERTY INVESTMENT FAR OUTWEIGH THE RISKS IF YOU KNOW WHAT TO DO.

go with the first insurance you see and figure that that will be enough, you are actually creating more risk for yourself—that of investing in the wrong coverage and wasting your money.

Why Should I Care?

I'm not worried. It's not going to happen to me.

This attitude has led many an investor into trouble. A worker hired to lay new carpet falls down stairs that are not up to code, and you get sued. A renter leaves a door open, and a skunk gets in, leaving a scent that costs thousands of dollars to remove. A storm blows a tree over. A sewer line breaks. A contractor you hired uses a blowtorch to get rid of a wasp nest on a porch instead of a can of insect spray and ends up burning down the whole house (true story!).

Are you sure you will be able to recover?

Sure. You have a policy. That's what insurance is for. Right?

Well, sometimes. But it's far more complicated than that.

The truth of the matter is that your insurance needs as an investor are just as unique and challenging as the properties you hold. Investment properties are considered higher risk by the industry than a typical homeowner's product. The reality is that a tenant is more likely to burn down a rental property than you are to burn down your own home. A vacant building is more likely to be vandalized than one that is occupied. And a property under construction is more likely to have accidents.

So it's a bit more difficult for you to find the right coverage simply due to the category you are in. The common perception that insurance companies just jack their rates up every year and that customers will never get any money out of them is valid to a small degree. Some carriers do have an automatic rate increase of 2–4 percent year over year built into their policies—not all, though. And as for the idea that you have to go to extremes to get companies to pay out, that really is a matter of the coverage you have. People tend to forget that insurance companies are just that—companies. They have to make money to stay in business. It is becoming increasingly difficult to do that for a number of reasons, fraud being just one.

But like every industry, there will always be a handful of people who will attempt to do anything to try to beat the system. And those bad apples make it challenging for the rest of us.

Why Should I Listen to You?

I certainly didn't go into this industry because it was going to make me popular. I know that insurance agents are not necessarily the most respected and sought-after people in the marketplace. We definitely aren't known for our celebrity status. Most times it is quite the opposite. We're lumped in with used car salesmen and carnival barkers. (Remember Ned Ryerson from *Groundhog Day*?)

Like you, I have paid my dues and taken my knocks. At one point I realized there was no such thing as a one-size-fits-all policy for real estate investors, and no company was adequately addressing the needs of this niche market. It took me too long to come to that revelation.

I did things the hard way, but I'm better off for it. In my youth, I dedicated my life to baseball; it's all I ever thought I'd do. I had huge dreams of making it to "the show," but it wasn't in the cards for me. Begrudgingly, I had to play the hand I was dealt. Part of that included a car accident my junior year in high school that effectively ended my baseball career, although I didn't realize it for a few years.

A drunk driver ran a red light (speeding, of course) at the busiest intersection in my hometown at rush hour, slamming into my Mustang

GT I'd worked so hard to buy when I got my license. It totaled my car and, worse than that, did significant damage to my right shoulder that required surgery and a long and extensive rehab. My baseball swing would never recover, and to this day I have constant pain in my right shoulder and down my arm. Fortunately for me I'm a leftie.

Despite this, I signed to play baseball in college at a small Division III school in Greencastle, Indiana (yeah, I'd never heard of it either), called DePauw University. But, like many other times in my life when I chose the hard way, I decided that having all of my college paid for was too easy, and I left DePauw. I fumbled around for a bit—went to a junior college the following year to try to save my baseball dreams—but in the end, it wasn't meant to be. My swing was never the same after the accident and surgery, and I'd missed too much time during rehab to catch up. I had to come up with plan B.

Fast-forward a few years, and I found myself back in school at Indiana University (not playing baseball) and married with a son. I was working multiple jobs and barely getting by. I ran into an acquaintance at Best Buy (next door to JCPenney, which was job number three for me at the time) who was loading several high-ticket electronics into his $100,000 SUV. So, of course, I asked him what he was doing, and when he told me, my whole way of thinking started to change. A couple of days later, we met for lunch, and he explained that he owned a few insurance agencies and offered me a job.

I didn't want to work in the home and auto industry (which were the types of accounts his agencies were mostly comprised of), but commercial real estate immediately stuck out to me. He and I started an independent agency that focused predominantly on large apartment complexes everywhere in the country. We invested $10,000 and purchased the contact information of apartment owners and property management companies all around the region.

I started "smiling and dialing," and that was the beginning of my career.

I'm no longer partners with him, and we've long since gone our separate ways, but I do credit him with getting me started. I would've never entertained the idea of working in the insurance industry if it hadn't been for him.

I'll admit that, in the beginning I was only in it for money, but that didn't last long. Right off the bat, I met a guy who is still a client today. He nearly got destroyed on a property claim because his insurance agent at the time didn't explain to him the limitations of his coverage and how it would affect him following a loss. The details of his case will come in a later chapter, but I watched as he only recovered about $28,000 from what should have been $250,000 because of all the things he got dinged for. He was underinsured, he had coinsurance, and his deductibles were too high.

I thought to myself, "What the hell is going on?!"

I started having every new client send me their existing policy so I could do a comparison for them. I didn't just read the policies; I actually did a line-by-line comparison. It takes probably three to four hours of work on a very simple one just to be able to go back and say, "Hey, here's where they're better. Here's where we're better. And this is why you should go with us."

It was really exciting stuff to read over and over again for thousands of hours. But it's how I taught myself about insurance policies and how to identify trapdoors that could harm my clients. The more I read into some of these insurance policies, the more disgusted I was at the state of affairs in the industry. I developed a passion for insurance that I never expected, and it set the stage for me to move into the insurance program space.

The industry had to change. Somebody had to bring logic back, and since nobody else seemed to be able or willing, I figured it might as well be me.

I started putting everything into it. By this time I had two young kids and was working full time at insurance during the day and then two jobs at night. Then, on the weekends, I'd work fifteen-hour days for my cousin who owned a landscaping company, trimming hedges and cutting grass. That was what it took to stay afloat.

> **THE INDUSTRY HAD TO CHANGE. SOMEBODY HAD TO BRING LOGIC BACK, AND SINCE NOBODY ELSE SEEMED TO BE ABLE OR WILLING, I FIGURED IT MIGHT AS WELL BE ME.**

I assume it's safe to guess that because you are reading this book, you understand what it means to work hard to get what you want. Admittedly I'm a workaholic, so part of me enjoyed it, but I was driven by a mission to take care of my family. I made a promise to my wife that I would provide for her and our children, and I stuck to my promise.

Eventually the burden started to lift. I cut down to just one job, and we were able to have some money in the bank—not a huge amount, but we were paying bills and doing okay.

After some time passed, my name was getting out there, and instead of just brokering one-off deals, I started building programs. This was where the revelation really started to hit me, and I realized how impactful my profession could be. I learned how to build programs for the benefit of investor clients, and a whole world opened up.

By this time I had joined with Tim Norris, the founder of NREIG, who had also found this niche in the market with real estate investors that a lot of the insurance companies didn't want to deal with. They obviously thought investors were kind of a pain in the butt because, well, you know how it is.

Here's how it works. Investors will buy a property that is occupied. Two months later the tenant will move out, and the investor needs to renovate it. And that means a policy will have to be canceled and replaced by a whole new policy, which brings a slew of paperwork for little money.

We decided to build a program that would allow us to make changes on a monthly reporting form according to our clients' changing needs. To make it work as close to real time as possible, we invented a pay-as-you-go plan that could accommodate locations through all phases of occupancy. We gave the investor all the power back to assess their needs and to notify us when a change happens in occupancy. This streamlined the process to where it became just a flip of a switch for us.

That's where it got interesting, because nobody else was doing anything like this at the time. Still to this day, you can't find anyone else who works like we do on a national level. That's the secret sauce that has made us who we are. My goal in writing this book is not to brag about the success of NREIG. I am writing it because I recognize I am in a unique position to observe the needs of real estate investors, and I have developed a set of guidelines I am happy to share with anyone who is interested in them. As an investor myself, this is the book I always wish I'd had.

There Is a Better Way

Maintaining your insurance should take seconds out of your life every month, not hours—or even minutes. With a well-educated guide to walk you through the process, you really shouldn't have to worry about insurance at all. Most companies in the insurance industry might see you as a high-maintenance customer and make you feel like they don't want to touch you, much less be in business with you.

That is wrong. You deserve to be valued and treated with the same amount of care and respect as every other customer. It is not your fault that they don't have the correct system in place to serve your needs.

Granted, as I mentioned, insuring your investment properties is a higher risk to insurance companies than insuring your personal residence. If you do get a carrier that decides that they'll take the added risk on, they're going to require an investor client like you to pay for a full year of premium up front, regardless of your intent and exit plan for the location. This is harmful to you, because there are several factors that can impact your insurance costs and coverages monthly.

Let's assume that when you purchased your insurance policy on your investment property, the location was occupied. The insurance company you went under contract with completed its underwriting process and rated the property as an occupied location.

Now let's fast-forward a few months, and your tenant has moved out—what do you need to do, and how much time and money will this cost you to complete? You contact your insurance agent, who tells you that they'll have to cancel your existing policy and replace it with either a vacant or builder's risk policy (if you need to renovate), and that policy has to be paid in full at inception as well. But they'll take their sweet time getting your money to you when it's their turn to pay you the refund due back to you for the policy previously in force that was canceled.

Here's the kicker—you'll be waiting for the refund of your unused premium from your first policy for up to sixty days, but you'll need to pay the premium for your new policy almost immediately. And every time the occupancy status changes, you get to repeat this cycle. It's a cash flow game, and if you don't have enough on hand right away, that can make it tricky. This is why a monthly reporter and a pay-as-you-go system is so valuable. We built this business to help investors acquire more properties. I'm not stupid enough to think it's just insurance costs that allow you to do that. But it makes it a lot easier when you're paying $50 a month on insurance instead of $600 up front for a year.

Now let's talk about a property you acquire to renovate and flip. These builder's risk policies are often "fully earned" at inception. This means when you buy the insurance policy, you buy it for that term. So if you buy a six-month policy, you pay six months up front. If you buy a year, you pay a year. But if you flip that property early, you need to cancel your insurance policy, because you don't have insurable interest anymore. However, in this scenario, the insurance company's not going to refund you the difference. You lose it. They collected a higher premium because they felt it was a higher risk, and then they came back to you and said, "If you flip it early, that's great. Let us know. But you're not getting any of your money back."

Simply put, regardless of the situation, you have no ability to recover any unused premium if you cancel the policy prior to its expiration. To avoid this you have to know how long you're anticipating your project will take to complete and somehow avoid buying a policy for a longer commitment than that. These policies are much easier to extend (if your project runs into delays) than they are to cancel prior to the expiration date.

> **Tip #1:** Builder's risk policies are almost always written as property coverage only. You may need to specifically request that liability be included to have liability coverage at the location.

Our national insurance program grew out of real-life frustration. As investors ourselves, Norris and I recognized many unique insurance challenges in our space, and we didn't want our investor clients going through the same thing. There are countless seemingly insignificant factors that add up to a huge difference, such as having pollution coverage included on your liability form that would cover you if you're sued by your tenant for carbon monoxide poisoning. That important coverage was excluded from every liability form for investors when we first got started.

We thought through things like this to protect our investors because (knock on wood) we would never have to worry about it. You know how it is. As soon as I strip that from my policy form, what's the first claim I'm going to see? It's going to be carbon monoxide poisoning.

> **Tip #2:** The general contractor's liability coverage is *not* sufficient to cover all liability exposures that exist at a location, despite what some of these general contractors may tell you.

Investor clients deserve the ability to get what they actually need without drastically inflating their coverage costs. A typical homeowner's policy includes meteors and volcanoes. Do you really need to cover that if you're only holding the property for a few months? Most likely not.

However, for something that poses a real threat or risk at your property, such as a dog bite (which, by the way, can get super expensive if a child is involved), most policies want to exclude real exposures like that. Sure, the insurance company is trying to minimize risk, just like investors are. And yet they'll include coverage for a meteor.

It's your property, and you have the right to do whatever you want with it. But you know as well as I do that a million things can happen. You have to be covered when it does. No—strike that. You have to be covered well *before* it does. Someone trespasses across the yard, trips on a hole, and sues you for a broken ankle. You activate your policy at 12:45 p.m., but then it turns out the accident happened at 11:00 a.m. You're toast.

This book's purpose is to help you think ahead and make the educated choices right now so that you can get back to doing what you really want to do—invest in real estate.

> **THIS BOOK'S PURPOSE IS TO HELP YOU THINK AHEAD AND MAKE THE EDUCATED CHOICES RIGHT NOW**

There is a better way. Companies like NREIG know that there are all kinds of tweaks and caveats that can be built into the forms to protect you, the investor. And the beauty is that they can be arranged in a way that also protects the insurance company. It's a win-win for everyone.

CHAPTER RECAP

Insurance isn't the big, scary monster that so many people believe it to be. It was set up to help people recover from loss after something unforeseen and damaging occurs, but, as businesses, insurance companies have to balance the risks they take when they promise coverage.

You can find a policy for almost anything that you value, especially if the loss would affect your livelihood or quality of life. For real estate investors, insurance is the best way to protect your assets with confidence. You are not locked into the same policy as every other investor. Your needs and values are unique, so your insurance should be customized to fit.

As you continue to read, you will learn how to advocate for yourself in the insurance space and make the most educated decisions that will save you money and allow you to sleep at night knowing that you have somewhere to turn if the worst happens.

EXERCISE—CHAPTER 1

Before we continue, this is a good time to ask yourself how satisfied you are with your current insurer. If they have been doing a great job, good for you! If you aren't sure, this is your chance to start thinking about what that would look like to you.

How many times have you shopped around for insurance for your real estate portfolio? Take a minute to research companies in your area and online that could potentially serve your needs. In the following chapters, you will find questions that you can ask your current insurance broker.

PROPERTY INSURANCE COMPANIES IN MY AREA	ONLINE PROPERTY INSURANCE COMPANIES

CHAPTER 2

WHAT DO I REALLY NEED TO KNOW?

In terms of weather and climate disasters, 2017 was a historic year, with sixteen massive events including three major hurricanes (Harvey, Irma, and Maria), eight severe storms, two major floods, a crop freeze, drought, rampant wildfires, a firestorm, and mudslides. Insurance companies were estimated to have paid out more than $130 billion in catastrophe losses. The following year wasn't much better, with close to $100 billion paid out for similar losses. This is stunning when you consider that, from 2000 to 2016, the average total insurance payout for disasters was about half that: $56 billion per year.[4]

One of the things you really need to know about insurance is that there are various parties involved in every transaction. It's easy to think that the person you write your checks out to (or the person who gets your electronic transfers) is the sole source of all things *insurance*

---

4   "Insure Natural Disaster Losses in 2017 Were 38% of Economic Costs of $353B: Aon, *Insurance Journal*, January 28, 2018, https://www.insurancejournal.com/news/international/2018/01/24/478246.htm

in your life. This is never the case. There are many people involved at many different levels, and they are easily confused. You've seen the words "carrier," "insurer," "agent," and "broker," but do you know what they actually mean?

This comes up all the time with our clients. I'm not going to define everything here. There is a handy glossary in the back for that. For the purposes of this chapter, it's important that you know that the "carrier" and the "insurer" are pretty much the same. Those words simply refer to the entity that will provide the insurance to the customer, the organization that will make decisions about what is covered and what is not. When there is a loss, the carrier/insurer will be the one who determines how much money will be compensated for the damages.

The "agent" or "broker" is the person who represents that company. They connect the customer with the carrier/insurer and can give advice on policies, process, and coverage options. It is important to understand the difference between a captive agent (who only works with one carrier, such as State Farm, for example) and an independent agent (who works with multiple carriers to get the best coverage and cost). Brokers are similar to agents, but their focus is researching and identifying the best companies and policies for their clients, with an in-depth knowledge of what every insurance company can offer.

Side note: NREIG is not an insurer/carrier. We represent both the carriers and our clients equally. We are tasked with protecting our carrier partners and providing them with good, profitable business while providing our clients with the most comprehensive and cost-effective coverage options from reputable insurance companies.

Prior to 2017, many insurance companies were considered "all in" in the habitational insurance market. The term "habitational space" when it comes to property insurance refers to single-family to large apartment buildings/complexes, condominiums, and multiunit dwellings (typically reserved for five or less units in a building) that generate income for the owners from people living on the property. This does not include office, retail, storage, or other nonresidential properties.

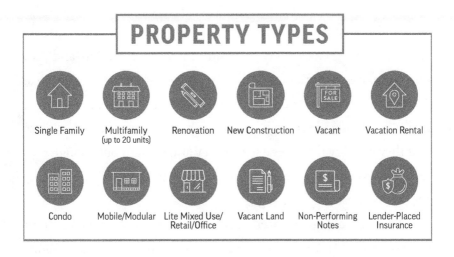

Single Family | Multifamily (up to 20 units) | Renovation | New Construction | Vacant | Vacation Rental

Condo | Mobile/Modular | Lite Mixed Use/ Retail/Office | Vacant Land | Non-Performing Notes | Lender-Placed Insurance

After 2017, many insurance companies had to stop and reevaluate their commitment to serve that market demographic.

Insurance companies actually forecast what they expect to pay in losses over a year based on historical data, and they look at how much they have in current written premium and projected growth. In other words, they do their best to guess how much they could be paying out to customers and plan accordingly. But when something happens that couldn't have been factored into the forecast, they find themselves suddenly paying out far more than expected. The only way to stay in business is for rates to go up. They always pass along to the end buyer. Staying in business means the outflow of money doesn't overtake the inflow.

It's no different than inflation in that regard. For example, if the cost of chicken feed suddenly rises due to drought, the price of eggs will go up in the grocery stores. Farmers and stores aren't going to take the loss; they're going to pass it along to the consumer. It's the same with insurance.

If one of the carriers NREIG works with insures all the properties in a given area for $250,000 but only collects $450 a year to cover those risks from those clients, how long do you think the insurance companies are going to stay in business if a hurricane hits and they have to pay out partial or full limits to every insured in that area? That's not a business model that can be sustained very long. Of course they want to provide enough benefit to the investor to be appealing so that they will buy the coverage. But they also want to put enough protective safeholds in place so that they can stay afloat. It's a balancing act that is constantly shifting.

By some estimates, premiums have gone up an average of 11 percent since 2017, and the number of insurance companies willing and able to provide coverage for the increasingly volatile habitational market has fallen. The number of carriers who can service policies for it is shrinking, and those who do continue to offer coverage are limiting their capacity because they are less willing to take on the risks they used to take.

Soft and Hard Markets

All of this adds up to the consumer being left with fewer options and less flexibility. This is called a "hardening" of the insurance market versus the state of a "soft" market. In a soft market, you can shop around every few months and often find a better deal because companies are in hot competition for your business. Soft markets mean lower premiums, broader coverage, more policies to choose from, and relaxed underwriters. Hard markets mean higher premiums, less coverage, fewer options to choose from, and harsher underwriters.

Here's a tip: underwriters are the people who study and assume potential risk, evaluate new insurance applications, and determine coverage

CONSUMERS ARE NOW LEFT WITH FEWER OPTIONS AND LESS FLEXIBILITY.

amounts. They are ultimately the ones responsible for determining whether to offer coverage on a given risk. They are also the ones who design the acceptable criteria for evaluating a risk, along with the company's actuaries.

When I started in the insurance industry in 2008, it was a soft market. Insurance companies were diving into the habitational space, eager to take advantage of big premiums, because they could make good money with small risk. Back then every deal was a dog fight because you had five or six other insurance companies and a handful of agents going after the same business.

Investors would leave for a savings of as little as five dollars; it was so volatile that way. The real estate market was good for investors, so people were buying left and right. Those of us in the insurance industry were nimbler, responding to fluctuations as needed, because we had the breathing room to do that.

Many fear that those days of easygoing, soft markets are long gone, but the trends have fluctuated in all parts of the insurance industry for ages. Seasoned insurance men and women take a less fearful approach, trusting in the old saying, "What goes up must come down." We know the market changes every forty-eight to seventy-two months, with drastic shifts happening usually every three to five years. If we are in a hard market and then go through a couple of calm hurricane and wildfire seasons, we'll expect a transition into a softer market over the next two years. We'll watch for companies to start jumping back into the game and trying to win more business.

THE INDUSTRY'S PREMIUM CYCLES

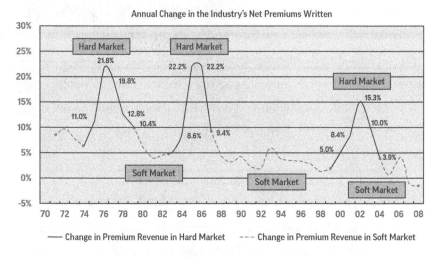

Figure 1 https://www.sec.gov/Archives/edgar/data/1453820/000095012309071916/
w76669exv99w1.htm

I always tell my investors to shop around every couple of years, even if they're insured with me. This will keep me on my toes and help me to make sure I'm doing my job. But I'll admit that in a hard market, it's almost not worth it because conditions don't change enough to bother. In a hard market, if it costs sixty cents per hundred dollars of property coverage with my program, then more than likely it's probably sixty cents to sixty-five cents everywhere else. In a hard market, it's a better use of your time to focus on the coverage package you get for that cost and other benefits that come along with the policy and agent you choose.

The good news to you is that if you're an investor in the smaller residential real estate market on a one-to-four-family type of portfolio, you will usually be the last market to see those increases. The customers who absorb them first are bigger apartment complexes, commercial real estate warehouses, and even self-storage. Pretty much everything will increase across the board before we do.

I ALWAYS TELL MY INVESTORS TO SHOP AROUND EVERY COUPLE OF YEARS, EVEN IF THEY'RE INSURED WITH ME.

Types of Investors

In my experience, investors fall into three basic categories: buy and hold, fix and flip, and wholesale. Whether you are an old pro or this is your first foray into the world of real estate investment, chances are you'll recognize yourself in one of the following descriptions.

BUY-AND-HOLD INVESTORS

If you fall into this category, you are the investor that NREIG was founded to serve. You have a rental portfolio and intend to keep and rent it for a number of years as a source of income. You may even function as landlord over your properties.

The portfolio of the buy-and-hold investor can range from one property to hundreds, if not thousands. I work with people who have inherited a cozy house from Grandpa who have decided to hang on to it and try to generate some income from it as a rental. They do almost everything themselves and are learning as they go. I have also worked with investors who are a part of huge conglomerates based in major metropolitan areas. These folks go out and buy bulk properties all over the country with the plan to keep them as long as they can generate a profit from the tenants. They usually rely on property management companies to keep things running smoothly.

Most often, the buy-and-hold investors fall somewhere in between these two ends of the spectrum. The middle includes those investors who are gobbling properties up as soon as they hit the market. They might do some light renovation and then turn around and put tenants in as fast as possible. If a tenant leaves, they'll do a quick cosmetic rehab, turn around, and throw another tenant in there.

I find the buy-and-hold investor typically lives where they invest and is actively engaged in their community. They like to invest in their backyards where they can drive by their properties every day and have a relationship with their tenants. Because of their relationships locally, they're in tune with what it's going to take to reasonably repair damages, and they usually have resources available to them.

Usually buy-and-hold investors care about their tenants and are trying to do what they can to help keep things maintained and repaired. They are a part of real estate investor associations and do their research. If there is a claim, they want to have it taken care of as timely as possible with enough money for them to come out even and able to move to the next project. They know what they have, know what they need, and know how to get it done.

FIX-AND-FLIP INVESTORS

Some people call these investors the turn-and-burn crowd. These are the buyers who seem to always be actively acquiring property. They are usually also very local and, like the buy and holds, know where to find good bargains and often buy properties on site.

They acquire something new, renovate as quickly and efficiently as possible (hopefully not cutting corners), and then try to sell it to another investor, buyer, or homeowner.

The operating question is whether they're going to make money from their investment and how quickly that's going to happen. I understand this drive. In certain markets you do your first two or three flips, and you're starting to make some pretty good money. It also doesn't take too long, depending on the market.

If you were to look at our book of business in 2017 and 2018, it was a pretty healthy split between buy-and-hold and fix-and-flip. We probably had 60 percent of the former and 40 percent the latter. But in 2021, it was more like 90 percent buy and hold and 10 percent fix and flip. In part due to the COVID-19 pandemic, our flippers became accidental landlords because they couldn't sell anything off. The market just didn't allow it. They just kind of got into the groove and learned how to hold rather than flip.

For those who have gone back to flipping, they'll come to us for a policy as they renovate, and then we don't hear from them for two or three months. They'll suddenly surface and buy their next policy, and the pattern continues.

WHOLESALE INVESTORS

When I say wholesale, I mean investors who buy properties for as low a cost as they can and flip, but without the fix. I've seen wholesalers buy at noon and close at five. That's how fast they can turn it. Wholesale's tricky because they may hold interest in the property for two hours, three days, or six weeks. There is so much variety in this group in that respect. But they all have one goal in common: selling to the end buyer right away to make a profit while spending as little as possible.

Every wholesaler is different. They make decisions based on where they are focused on growing their portfolio, expected ROI, size and value of the home, whether the property is rent ready or not, and other relevant factors. Wholesalers are some of our best clients. Sometimes they buy properties from other investors or from foreclosures. Sometimes they renovate a bit, and when they sell a property to an investor, they offer to be the property manager and stay on because they have an interest from the get-go. They know where the good neighborhoods are and watch them carefully for opportunities. They'll take a liking to a certain location, knowing it can bring high revenue.

From the insurance standpoint, they will typically only buy liability coverage because, if even one catastrophe happens in that four- or five-hour window, it could ruin everything. The last thing they need is for someone to trip and fall and sue them while they are minutes away from handing the keys over to the new owners.

As you can imagine, there is no absolute line separating these three groups. One of our best clients falls into all three categories simultaneously. She has a group that will buy properties in bulk—maybe twenty or thirty at a time. They will often sell off a portion right away (for a profit, of course!), fix others up before they sell, and keep the rest in the rental portfolio. This group will also approach new buyers of the properties they like and offer to stay on as a landlord or property manager for a fee. Not a bad way to run a business if you ask me.

Appetite for Risk

When it comes to claims, the loss conversation is very different from one group to the next because their risk appetites are different. Buy-and-hold investors tend to be more conservative in nature because they are investing for the long term. They are not looking to make a quick buck, but rather want to make the most judicious decisions they can. We talk to them about their experience in the business and their intent for the property. We ask questions like, "What kind of area is your portfolio in? Do you have tenants lined up? Are there renovations coming?"

Flippers, on the other hand, sometimes tend to be more flippant (see what I did there?) about their insurance. When a loss happens, the two driving questions become, "How much does making the repairs interrupt my plans for the location?" and "Can I still make the same (or near same) amount of money on the flip once the repairs are complete?"

LEVEL OF EXPERIENCE OFTEN PLAYS A KEY ROLE IN GAUGING APPETITE FOR RISK.

If it's a larger loss, they will ask, "Is it going to make more sense for me to clear the lot and sell it? Or am I going to have to expend resources of my own to try to make all this work and sell it after that?" Profit is king with these folks.

Level of experience often plays a key role in gauging appetite for risk. Let's say a nice young couple with two babies just inherited Great-Aunt Bessie's cabin in the woods. They decide to keep it and turn it into a vacation rental. Now imagine a professional contractor who moonlights as a real estate investor comes in and buys a cabin right next door. A major windstorm knocks trees onto the roofs of the two cabins. The contractor has a crew on standby with chainsaws and power tools ready to fix the roof as soon as the storm passes. He can confidently say to his broker, "See, I didn't need a lot of coverage because I can fix this myself and absorb the cost."

The young couple, on the other hand, may barely have enough money in their bank account to pay their own bills, much less to cover the cost of fixing their cabin's roof. And that doesn't even address the knowhow, resources, or time that would be required to do that work themselves. In other words the payout from the insurance claim is the only way they can make the property whole again.

As insurance brokers, we want to know what your exit strategy is. If you have a partial loss, what does that mean? If you have a total loss, what are the plans? Do you have substantial cash flow, and do you have a line of potential renters waiting to rent from you? That's very different than somebody who says, "If I have a partial loss, I'll probably just sell the property as is and go buy another one like it. If it burns to the ground, I'll clean up the rubble, sell the land, and move on." Those are very different needs that require a different set of insurance coverages, and there are all kinds of intricacies and unique perspectives to consider.

Maybe you have owned your properties outright and have never filed a property claim. You're smart enough to do that math and say, "You know what? I paid a whole lot for insurance over the years with no insurance claims. Not saying a fire won't happen, but it hasn't to me. So if you look at all the money I paid in premiums over the years, if I had just self-insured my property, I would have an extra $180,000. I could have bought three more properties with that!"

You wouldn't be wrong in thinking that, and there's nothing wrong with that line of thinking. There is no right or wrong way to do this. There are many good and not-so-good options available, and you get to decide which path to take.

Exit Strategy

In the end it really comes down to the goals you have for your real estate investment. We call this the exit strategy. If you are a buy-and-holder, you probably don't have a plan to exit. That's inherent in the name—hold. You need a plan that will serve you well in the event of a loss but won't drain you dry with high premiums.

If you are a flipper, you are trying to move that property along, so you need a policy that suits your needs. If you suffer a partial or total loss, you have to decide if you would want to rebuild or not, and your insurance plan should accommodate that decision. You also need an insurance company that is as nimble as you are. If you are planning to flip that property in three months, you certainly don't want to be locked into a year-long commitment—especially if you're going to be buying a whole new policy on a new property as soon as you can.

> **IT ALL COMES DOWN TO THE GOALS YOU HAVE FOR YOUR REAL ESTATE INVESTMENT.**

And if you are a wholesaler, you may decide (after discussing with your agent) that you do not need property insurance at all (don't confuse this with not needing liability coverage, though, which we'll tackle later), but it depends on your preferences and appetite for risk as well as how long you will have ownership interest in the property.

Lender Requirements

If your lender has insurance requirements, the factors just mentioned may be moot. Lenders require certain things from their investors before they will do business with them, and one of those is for the insurance to meet or exceed certain requirements. They are not willing to take a risk on giving you money until they know that you're adequately insured.

This is one of the most commonly missed steps for new investors when they begin to get into this space. They forget to ask their lender what the requirements are and end up having delays at the closing table. It happens all the time.

When you look at insurance lending requirements on private and hard money lenders or traditional lending institutions, it's different from your typical homeowner's policy. These are often commercial loans, so when they lend on their investment portfolios, they want very broad, comprehensive coverages to minimize or completely eliminate any risk that they have of a claim potentially going uncovered.

On my end it's necessary for carriers with an appetite in this space to be flexible on the coverage forms that they offer investors because it's largely by what the lender requires. So if you partner with an agent who has access to more than one or two markets, that will help ensure that they're going to be able to provide the flexibility you need.

I get it. Your livelihood is at stake here. So is my job. You've got a million things on your plate. Acquiring property insurance is the last thing on your mind, but if you neglect it, you're going to have unexpected roadblocks on deals. And if you're not partnering with the right agent, you'll get to a closing table to try to buy a property and discover too late that it doesn't meet requirements. So ask that question before you buy. I know—it seems counterintuitive to ensure you have adequate insurance coverage in line for the home you're closing on ahead of the closing happening. You don't even own it yet, but trust me. It's the smart way to do things.

Here is an example of a typical lending requirement page you might see. When you break it down bullet by bullet, it's not really that complex. I encourage you to take a few minutes to read through this and figure out what each one means in your specific situation:

Insurance Lending Requirements

SHAWN'S PRIVATE LENDING SERVICES

Property

- **Settlement method:** Replacement Cost is required, with the insured building value being the amount of the loan, at minimum.

- **Coverage Form:** Special form property coverage is required. Basic or Broad coverage forms are not acceptable.

- **Coinsurance:** Policy must not include a coinsurance clause.

- **Deductible:** The maximum AOP (all other perils) property deductible allowed is $5,000. Exceptions are allowed for the perils of Wind/Hail, Named Windstorm, and Theft and VMM (Vandalism & Malicious Mischief) if needed.

- **Named Windstorm (Hurricane) coverage** must be included for all locations located in a tier 1 or 2 county. The maximum deductible allowed for the peril of Named Windstorm is 3% of the total insured value at the location, or the AOP property deductible, whichever is greater.

- **Loss of Rents coverage** is required for all occupied locations.

- **Flood coverage** is required if the property is located in a high hazard flood zone.

- **Earthquake coverage** is required if the property is located along the New Madrid fault line, or in the following states (CA, WA, OR, AK, HI) earthquake coverage is required.

- Coverage must be written by a carrier rated "A" or better by A.M. Best

- Shawn's Private Lending must be listed as Mortgagee and Lenders Loss Payable as follows:

  Shawn's Private Lending Services, LLC
  ISAOA/ATIMA
  246 Main St.
  Kansas City, MO, 64153

Liability

- **Premises Liability** coverage must be obtained with the minimum coverage limits of $1,000,000 per occurrence and a $2,000,000 annual policy aggregate limit, per location. No shared limit policies are permitted.

- Personal Liability policies are not acceptable.

- **Deductible:** Maximum liability deductible allowed is $2,500

- If the location is undergoing renovation and the borrower is a General Contractor and completing the renovation themselves, either a General Liability policy must be obtained (in lieu of the Premises Liability coverage) with no exclusion for Products and Completed Operations, or the borrower must provide proof of coverage for their General Contractor's Liability in addition to their Premises Liability coverage.

- For locations exceeding three stories, an additional $1,000,000 of liability coverage per story is required in the form of an excess liability or umbrella policy (due to the change in means of egress).

- Shawn's Private Lending must be listed as Additional Insured on the Premises Liability policy as follows:

  Shawn's Private Lending Services, LLC
  ISAOA/ATIMA
  246 Main St.
  Kansas City, MO, 64153

Please feel free to shop your Insurance with National Real Estate Insurance Group at NREIG.com

Never Give an Insurance Company a Reason to Decline a Claim

Insurance is for sudden and unforeseen damage. That's what it's there for. But over time it has gained a reputation for being a big, bad, money-making scam that doesn't actually do anyone any good. This has to do largely with claims and the way they are handled with clients

PROBABLY THE BIGGEST MISCONCEPTION WITH CLAIMS OVERALL IS THAT CARRIERS AND THEIR ADJUSTERS WANT TO DENY EVERY CLAIM.

when any sudden and unforeseen damage takes place. It's also due in part to how we as agents (not all of us) have neglected the importance of educating our clients on every part of their insurance contract and discussing coverage options thoroughly.

Often, claims go to an insurance adjuster who either works for the insurance company/carrier or for a third-party adjusting firm (or TPA). Many companies use third-party firms as local boots-on-the-ground decision makers if they offer national coverage.

> **Side note:** In our program, the TPA we work with most often is McLarens Global. Nick Thompson and his team in Oklahoma City are the best in the business. They provide an enormous value to our clients, our carrier partners, and my team.

Probably the biggest misconception with claims overall is that carriers and their adjusters want to deny every claim. This is completely wrong. Believe it or not, they absolutely, 100 percent of the time want to pay the claim (when warranted). It's true!

The head of our Client Experience department, Jason Jones, whose background was in claims for many years, handled thousands of claims prior to coming to NREIG. He said of his time as an adjuster,

> When I was adjusting claims, the ones that were painful were the ones that I had to deny. When we could go out and pay the claim, everybody's happy. It goes away, and we don't have extra work to do. As the agent now, we're rooting for you, not against you. When the carrier has to deny you, that's a difficult spot for the adjuster and for the agent. We would really like to help, but when we can't it's almost always because the person who filed the complaint didn't understand their policy or didn't know what they actually had.

This brings me to the advice I always give: never give an insurance company a reason to deny your claim.

NAMED INSURED

So many investors have business names that they use interchangeably. Let's say my insurance policy is under my name, Shawn Woedl, but my tenants pay rent to my entity that actually owns the

NEVER GIVE AN INSURANCE COMPANY A REASON TO DENY YOUR CLAIM.

property, which I call SW, LLC. If one of my tenants slips down the stairs and breaks their leg, they're going to sue SW, LLC, because that's where they pay their rent. If my LLC is not listed on my policy, and that claim comes in, there's no coverage. I'm toast.

This also becomes a problem when people change their entity name but forget to update it on their insurance policy. The first named insured on the insurance policy always needs to be the entity that purchased the property, so if you purchased it as an LLC, the LLC needs to be listed as the named insured. To put it simply, make sure whatever entity (personal or business) owns the property is the first named insured on your policy.

OCCUPANCY STATUS

Reporting occupancy status changes to your insurance company is critical to maintaining proper coverage at all times. Most importantly occupancy status must be accurate at the time of loss. In general a property would fall into one of these occupancy types:

- Occupied: Property currently occupied by a tenant or will be occupied by tenants within sixty days. If a property has been vacant for more than sixty days but has been reported as occupied, coverage may be diminished. These vacancy provisions are different with every carrier, so be sure to review your policy or ask your agent to confirm (some may only provide thirty days to report a change in occupancy, as an example).
  - Owner occupied: When the owner of the property lives at the property with a homeowner's insurance policy.
  - Tenant occupied: When the property is occupied by renters with a landlord policy.
    - Note: This is the focus of NREIG services.
- Renovation: Currently undergoing renovation or within sixty days of completion. Claims on these properties are settled on invested capital at the time of loss. This includes both cosmetic and structural renovations.

- Vacant: Not undergoing renovation and not occupied. Frequently such properties are on the market for sale sixty days after rehab is complete. Vacant properties must be locked and secured at all times. Failure to do so may affect coverage in the event of a loss.

- New construction: A dwelling being built from the ground up.

INSURABLE INTEREST

Insurable interest is a legal concept that basically means you must have financial or other interest in the claimed, damaged property to be eligible for reimbursement by your insurance coverage. It might seem simple at first, but it can be a big problem when the person who is insured does not actually own the property.

For instance if you were the one who inherited Great-Aunt Bessie's cabin in the woods, don't take for granted that her original homeowner's policy is going to cover you. Great-Aunt Bessie's homeowner's policy won't cover you because you are not the named insured on her policy, and since *she* no longer has insurable interest in the property, she can't hold the insurance on it.

Basically if you've taken ownership but haven't obtained insurance in your or your owning entity's name and the house burns to the ground, Aunt Bessie's policy (if still in force) isn't paying a dime on the loss. In addition, if you rent Aunt Bessie's cabin to tenants, the tenants can't insure the property because they have no insurable interest in it either. They don't own it, so they can't get paid on a claim for damage.

CHAPTER RECAP

As you try to make sense of all the information and options available to you, it is important to remember that there is no single right or wrong way to insure your investments. Factors such as hard/soft market conditions, investing goals, tolerance for risk, and lender requirements play a significant role in the decisions around which policies are best suited for your investment portfolio. Once you have settled on the best coverage, there are steps you can take to increase the chances that future claims will not be denied. Being the first named on the policy, reporting occupancy status, and clarifying insurable interest are crucial in these circumstances.

EXERCISE—CHAPTER 2

Before you read the next chapter, look at the chart below to determine what kind of investor you are, considering your experience and your appetite for risk. If you have more than one property, consider making a list of the properties in your real estate investment portfolio and writing down the goals and exit strategies for each one.

	BUY & HOLD	FIX & FLIP	WHOLESALING
Do you want to build a larger portfolio of properties to develop wealth over time?	X		
Do you want to be a landlord and manage tenants?	X		X
Are you looking for shorter-term deals for quicker profit?		X	X
Are you willing to put some sweat into a fixer upper?	X	X	
Are you interested in being the middle man by acquiring properties to immediately sell to another buyer?			X

IN CASE YOU ARE WONDERING: WHAT MAKES INSURANCE RATES GO UP, ANYWAY?

Factors Affecting Rates

It doesn't take major events like named hurricanes to harden the market. Even a particularly bad year of wind and hail can impact it. Rate-increasing events can occur locally, regionally, or nationally. In February 2021, a freak winter storm hit Texas, and suddenly everyone was filing claims on frozen pipes and the resulting water damage. No big surprise that the property market hardened there practically overnight. All it takes is one bad season and a string of uncontrollable losses, and things tighten up.

If you invest in areas where major catastrophes have not impacted the market and your recent loss history is good, then your rate increases should be minimal year over year. On the other hand, if you invest in areas that are more volatile such as California, Texas, Louisiana, and Florida, you could see increases anywhere from 10 to 70 percent.

Other factors that are beyond your control include the following:

- Insurance company preference: Some companies (not the ones that power our program) have a rate increase built in that automatically takes it up 2 to 4 percent year over year. That's more common in the homeowner's market than in the real estate investment side of things, but it's not unheard of.

- Inflation: Not much we can say or do about this one. It happens. It's a factor. Enough said.

- Geographic area: Insurance in New York is not the same as insurance in Sarasota, in Houston, or in Kansas City. Some areas of our country are simply more prone to natural disaster. Some are at a higher risk for crime. And some have tougher climates. Insurance companies know the statistics better than probably anyone else, and they use that information as they create their policies and rating matrices for these policies. Don't be shocked if the apartment complex you buy in Milwaukee has much higher rates than the complex you own in Phoenix. Carriers know the area, and they know what to expect in terms of typical claims. They also know the demographics they serve, and they adjust their policies accordingly.

- Carrier history: An aggressive new insurance company in this space can have many benefits in terms of exciting ideas and forward-thinking staff, but they may not have the ability to absorb the same kinds of losses that a large, well-established one can. As with any type of business, you can find both in the insurance industry. These include those behemoths that have become household names such as Allstate, Farmers, and Liberty Mutual as well as those you may have never heard of. Inexperienced agents and underwriters play a role as well. We've seen instances where some companies got into trouble because they did not do their part at the underwriting stage and didn't understand the risks. This always comes back in the end. Well-established carriers will make decisions based on their experience in a specific area of the country. They may be tempted to increase the rates of all their clients by 20 percent across the board, and then they will look at their clients in places like Las Vegas, Phoenix, and Detroit and say, "We've had a whole lot of claims in those places specifically, so we're going to raise rates 50 percent there and keep everything else flat." They can do that because of their unique experience, which may actually be different from every other carrier in the market.

Factors Not Affecting Rates

Turning in claims shouldn't affect your rates if they aren't paid out (maybe the claim amount is under your deductible or the cause of loss is determined to be an excluded peril). But I want to add a disclaimer here that this pattern can affect your relationship with your carrier. If they find you to be high maintenance (meaning you're the type of person who wants insurance to handle every hangnail), you could be looking for a new carrier before long. For example, a string of loss frequency, even with no payout, can lead an insurer to wonder when the big one's going to hit, and they are going to be on the hook when it does.

All of this begs this question: With so much out of one's control, is there anything a savvy real estate investor *can* do to control insurance costs without jeopardizing coverage? The answer is yes!

> A PATTERN OF TURNING IN CLAIMS CAN AFFECT YOUR RELATIONSHIP WITH YOUR CARRIER.

Investor Impact/Role

One of the most important things you can do is take true ownership of your investments. If you have a string of claims that are considered controllable losses, then you will likely see an increase in your insurance company's effort to recover some of the money they paid out on those losses. Acts of God are treated differently, obviously, but controllable losses are the claims you want to try to stay away from. They drive insurance companies insane.

These claims can really impact your insurance premiums or jeopardize your ability to find replacement coverage. In this respect, frequency is as bad as severity. If you are constantly turning in insignificant claims that you could have prevented, it's just as bad as turning in one major one. It's death by a thousand cuts.

As for the worst offenders in terms of controllable losses, theft is a big one, followed by water damage. You also want to stay away from arson claims if at all possible. All of these can drive insurance companies crazy, because if an investor is managing their properties and businesses the right way, controllable losses can usually be avoided or at least minimized. If you have this problem, you can expect to see some pretty significant increases in your premiums.

Do your due diligence to prevent loss. The most preventable property losses we see include the following:

- Fire (from cooking and heating): For occupied properties, install and test smoke alarms monthly, install fire extinguishers, and install fire suppression systems. For unoccupied properties, layer security, make it look lived in, and recruit neighbors to watch for unwanted "guests."
- Water: Losses are most commonly caused by burst pipes during winter. To avoid, take measures such as insulating

pipes, teaching tenants to let water drip at night, monitoring thermostats, and knowing how to shut water off and drain the system.

- Theft: Theft is particularly prevalent with properties under renovation or for sale—specifically up to four times more common than other kinds of loss. Do everything you can to make the property look lived in, properly secure it by reinforcing doors, enlist neighbors to monitor, keep yards clean and trim, use exterior lighting, and install an effective alarm system. If needed, board up all openings.

- Tenant damage: Whether unintended or malicious, this is almost always preventable. The most common type of tenant damage is cooking fires, so be sure to take steps to reduce that risk in the kitchen. Usual wear and tear is normal and never covered by insurance, but when tenants leave, you may need to take additional steps to ensure there is no added loss such as theft of large appliances or damage to walls.

- Trees: Damage from trees is the source of tens of thousands of claims each year, some of which reach upward of $30,000 to $70,000 cost per claim to the investor. Check on the trees on your investment properties regularly, and keep them well trimmed.

- Liability: There is so much to say about this that I had to include a whole chapter about it later in the book. But to be brief, mindful maintenance and swift responses can reduce these claims to almost zero. Know what you're up against in terms of liability risk, and plan accordingly.

In the end I know that insurance seems like just one more expense to add to the million other expenses that come with real estate investment, and you want to get the most bang for your buck. That's exactly why I wrote this book. You don't want to spend more than you need, but at the same time, you want to be careful not to leave yourself open to risks that could end up costing you.

How do you do that, exactly? Unfortunately there is no simple answer. But it all starts with knowing what kind of investor you are and being clear about your goals.

CHAPTER 3

WHAT KIND OF COVERAGE DO I ACTUALLY NEED?

In March 2021 Texas was hit by a polar vortex that brought historic low temperatures, crippling the power grid statewide and bringing transportation and commerce to a halt. For good reason, structures in the southern United States are built to get rid of heat, not keep it in. That, coupled with the unprecedented nature of this event, brought on catastrophic consequences. After temperatures warmed back up, insurance companies were bombarded with claims for water damage from broken pipes. Many homes in Texas keep their water heaters in the attic, so families who fled their icy homes returned to find ceilings collapsed and rooms flooded.

The first thing they had to do was find out if they had coverage for this sort of damage. Insurance language is designed to confuse, but it's not impossible. If you have ever

THE FIRST CHOICE YOU HAVE WHEN PURCHASING A NEW PROPERTY POLICY IS WHAT KIND OF COVERAGE YOU NEED.

felt anxious about your insurance policy, take heart. Once you take the time to read and understand the policies, they are actually fairly simple to figure out. It's helpful to orient yourself first so that you know what you're looking at.

If you want adequate and appropriate coverage, for the most part, you need property and liability coverage at the very minimum. Every investor situation is different, depending on your investment strategy, but I think it's safe to assume you want to cover the dwelling.

The first choice you have when purchasing a new property policy is what kind of coverage you need. There are three options that investors have an opportunity to choose from: basic, special, and broad form.

The decision about which to use will be based on your unique exit strategy and appetite for risk—unless there's a lender on the deal, in which case your lender will choose for you, and it will always be special form. The basic form is just too stripped down.

But if you are in a position where you can choose, here's an overview that should help as you lay your options out and draw comparisons.

Basic Form

Basic form is a "named peril" policy. Think of it as a really stripped-down policy covering only the basics, as the name suggests. This means that if you want coverage, the peril has to actually be listed by name on the declarations page. If it's not specifically listed, there is no coverage afforded to you following a loss. Here's an example:

CAUSE OF LOSS	BASIC
Fire	☑
Lightning	☑
Explosion	☑
Windstorm and Hail	☑
Smoke	☑
Aircraft and Vehicles	☑
Riot or Civil Commotion	☑
Volcanic Action	☑
Sprinkler Leakage	☑
Vandalism / Malicious Mischief (Subject to Sublimit of $30,000)	☑
Falling Objects	
Weight of Snow, Ice or Sleet	
Water Damage	
Collapse - Additional Coverage	
Theft (Subject to Sublimit of $30,000)	
Risk of Direct Physical Loss (Subject to Policy Exclusions)	

From one company to another, these perils are pretty much the same everywhere you go. You may find a manuscripted (prebuilt) form that moves away from it a bit by excluding one of the perils, like vandalism for example. But for the most part, they're all the same. You'll rarely see a basic form policy that adds additional coverages; they will only pull from them.

It may go without saying that when choosing this coverage form, you want to be careful. Be absolutely certain that you're okay with these exact coverages and that you are comfortable self-insuring the causes of loss that are not covered.

As you make an educated decision about what's best for your portfolio, it can be tempting to go with basic when you can because there is about a 25 percent cost difference between special and basic.

It is appealing to save a quarter of your premium expenses annually on your insurance costs—as long as you are certain you can take care of perils that are not covered.

SELF-INSURED

This is a good time to define the term "self-insured." "Self-insured" simply means that you are financially able to pay for the costs of repairs of damages not covered by your insurance. If you're more of a risk taker or have plenty of resources available, self-insuring your property can be a viable option. Another way to think of this is in terms of the deductible that you carry. That is the amount of a loss you will never be able to recover.

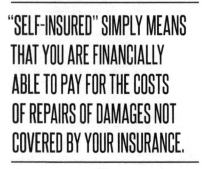

"SELF-INSURED" SIMPLY MEANS THAT YOU ARE FINANCIALLY ABLE TO PAY FOR THE COSTS OF REPAIRS OF DAMAGES NOT COVERED BY YOUR INSURANCE.

Not all investors purchase property coverage if it is a low-value property they paid for in cash, and they are comfortable self-insuring a property loss because the payout would not be very high. However, I recommend never, ever, ever going without liability coverage. We will go more into this in the liability chapter (because I can't stress this enough), but for the next few chapters, we'll be focusing on property coverage.

If you want to think of it in other terms, consider why some parents of teenage drivers might choose to get "liability only" rather than "full coverage." Perhaps they are really good at fixing cars and figure they can take a mallet to the dings and dents that inevitably appear. Or maybe they live in an area where the risk of car accidents is pretty slim. Or maybe the car is a decades-old beater, and they wouldn't bother fixing it in the first place. Regardless of the reason, liability coverage is sufficient for their needs, and it saves them money. But you never want to be caught without liability coverage in case your teen damages someone else's car or, worse, kills someone with that car.

FACTORS TO CONSIDER

Your decision is based on a number of factors, including where your investment portfolio sits geographically. Is there really a risk of exposure? Take "weight of snow, ice, or sleet" for example. Coverage for damages in this category are excluded on the basic form under coverage options available. If your property is in sunny Tampa or Phoenix, you may be good. But if it's in Kansas City or Missoula, you would probably be wise to consider a more comprehensive form of insurance (see special below).

Also, what stage of development is your property in? As you now know, an occupied property in a quiet neighborhood is at far less risk than one under construction in a largely unoccupied area in terms of risk of theft. If somebody rips the copper out of the walls or steals the AC unit, basic form insurance can't help you. This leads to a conversation about the deductible, which will come in a few chapters, but for now consider that if you have a high-value property under development, you'll need to decide if you are comfortable self-insuring it for theft. If you are, then basic may be a way for you to save some money, which could always be put toward buying a new AC unit, should you need it.

The most common confusion with special form, however, is the peril that's called "water damage." People think this means flood or backup of sewer and drains, but it doesn't. To be considered "water damage," the damage must come from an internal water source within the home, and it is not covered in basic form. Often this loss is accidental in nature, such as the pipes freezing and bursting. That kind of damage can add up quickly if it's not caught and controlled right away. Think about the flooring, the wiring, the wall coverings, the furniture, the possessions, and, in some cases, even the ceilings and light fixtures. If you think your property may be at risk for these kinds of incidents, it's probably good to reconsider special form over basic form.

BURDEN OF PROOF

The last element to consider with basic form insurance is where the burden of proof lies. This is a big thing to remember because, under a basic form policy, the insured and their agent always, *always* carry the burden to prove to the insurance company that whatever happened was caused by an included peril.

That can be difficult at times because there is quite a lot of gray area in there. Let's take vandalism and the difference between the two forms. "Vandalism/malicious mischief" is covered on both forms, but in order to get the "theft" coverage, you've got to buy special form. The problem is that those usually go hand in hand, right?

If I carry basic form and somebody kicks down the door to my house and rips all the copper out of the walls, a portion of that claim is not going to be covered. Anything that is stolen is not covered. The initial point of entry, however, is covered. If the vandals messed up your doorframe and the damage exceeds your deductible, fortunately that loss is covered. But the copper wire is not.

Special Form

As a broker, I don't tend to push investors in one direction or the other when it comes to which form to select, but, for the most part, I always explain that special form is safer. It really is the best option for most people, and because it is the most *extensive*, it is also the most *expensive* form an investor can purchase.

You know how it is. The first thing that happens after you purchase your basic form insurance policy is that a pipe bursts or your property is broken into and all of the copper wiring and appliances are stolen, and you're coming to me to make a claim. And then I have to remind you

I ALWAYS EXPLAIN THAT SPECIAL FORM IS SAFER.

that you bought basic form, and I can't help you. Then my hands are tied, and you're in a difficult financial position that could've been avoided. It's unfortunate for everyone.

If you have a lender on the deal, then it's a moot point. Lenders always require special form because they want no risk whatsoever. And rightfully so. A borrower is at higher risk of defaulting on their loan if they are in financial hardship due to an uncovered loss that occurred at their property that has to be paid out of their pocket to repair. Cash flow can get extremely tight.

CAUSE OF LOSS	BASIC	SPECIAL
Fire	☑	☑
Lightning	☑	☑
Explosion	☑	☑
Windstorm and Hail	☑	☑
Smoke	☑	☑
Aircraft and Vehicles	☑	☑
Riot or Civil Commotion	☑	☑
Volcanic Action	☑	☑
Sprinkler Leakage	☑	☑
Vandalism/Malicious Mischief (Subject to Sublimit of $30,000)	☑	☑
Falling Objects		☑
Weight of Snow, Ice or Sleet		☑
Water Damage		☑
Collapse - Additional Coverage		☑
Theft (Subject to Sublimit of $30,000)		☑
Risk of Direct Physical Loss (Subject to Policy Exclusions)		☑

ONE SIZE ALMOST FITS ALL

So my advice to pretty much everyone is that it's probably worth it to get special form. The expense is less of an issue if you have a monthly reporting system like the ones we use at NREIG. It's not as big of a deal. How much of a difference does 20 to 25 percent make when you're paying monthly instead of annually? When you break it out over twelve months, it's a little easier and a whole lot safer.

Special form used to be called "all risk" coverage. It's changed a bit, particularly in the case of policies designed for investors, but it's still the most comprehensive property coverage you can buy as an investor. The reason behind that is, unless the cause of loss is specifically excluded in your policy, coverage is afforded to you on special form following a loss.

That means you can rest assured you won't be denied unless what happens is specifically excluded or you did not abide by some element of the insurance contract, such as saying there are working smoke detectors in the house when there are none. And the burden of proof falls on the insurance company to prove the cause of loss is a stated exclusion instead of you proving it is covered. Remember, adjusters are on your side. They want to help you, and the special form allows them more flexibility in terms of claims being paid out.

Special form is also a good choice if your appetite for risk is fairly low because the risk to an investor is very minimal. If an investor comes to me and says, "I don't want to deal with anything. I want everything covered," I don't even bother to talk about basic. Special form is the best option I have for those investors.

Any licensed agent should know the difference between the two and be able to go over the differences for you in detail. You want to be careful, because just like on the basic form, there are manuscripted special form policies as well. You might find a policy that has a full theft exclusion buried in it that you don't find out about until it's too late. You don't want to feel like you're paying for that coverage and then not get it.

To avoid being insufficiently covered and risking a nasty surprise in the event of a loss, always find out about the exclusions that exist in every policy you consider.

Exclusions on Special Form

Exclusions are a standard part of insurance, and they all exist for a reason. The "mold and fungus" exclusion, for example, stemmed from something that took the insurance industry by storm. Back in the mideighties, mold and fungus weren't really talked about much, especially in the insurance community. Around the nineties, the medical and scientific community learned the danger of mold and fungus and set about making their findings very public. What resulted was an explosion of "toxic" or "black" mold claims that all had to be paid out. It rocked the entire insurance industry to its core. The industry responded by slamming exclusions into every existing policy faster than any exclusion in the history of insurance. Those claims took years to recover from.

Other exclusions like "wear and tear" and "intentional tenant damage" have emerged more organically over time as companies decided they didn't make sense. The following is a list of standard property exclusions you can always expect to see on any special form policy.

Standard Property Exclusions

In general, insurance provides coverage for many sudden, unforeseen, unintended, and unplanned events. Special form coverage protects property against any source of loss that is not specifically excluded. Causes of loss that are not covered on most policies are as follows:

- Mold and Fungus—some of our program carriers include limited mold coverage up to $15,000.
- Wear and Tear.
- Earth Movement (including earthquake and sinkhole)—can be purchased separately.
- Flood—can be purchased separately.
- Terrorism—included in your proposal unless you request to

> have it removed.
> - Sewer and Drain Backup—limited coverage can be purchased separately via our Tenant Protector Plan.
> - Intentional Tenant Damage (including, but not limited to, malicious destruction before and during occupancy, or within ten days of eviction or vacancy is excluded.)

Thankfully some of these exclusions can be bought back on a stand-alone policy, though not all of them. "Wear and tear" is uninsurable no matter what. It doesn't fall within the scope of sudden and unforeseen, and insurance isn't a maintenance plan, so you can't buy coverage for that. "Intentional tenant damage" is another one that is always excluded, but the market's changing. Right now you cannot buy coverage for it, but I wouldn't be surprised if this changes in the coming years. Many other countries have this coverage available, so international trends may have an impact.

Stand-alone policies won't solve every problem, but they can make a difference. Let's say you have a duplex in Charleston, South Carolina, and you know from your research that it is actually one of the most earthquake-prone cities in the country. Even though earthquakes have been pretty mild historically, you're not comfortable leaving it to chance. You can purchase an earthquake policy to cover your property in the event a more substantial event occurs. And you can sleep a bit better at night. That's what really matters.

Broad Form

At NREIG we don't even offer broad form because there's not much reason to do so. It's so close to special form. There is only one coverage difference (theft), and the price difference is so minimal that it doesn't make sense to buy it. I counsel everyone who is considering broad form to just go with the special form. As a matter of fact, most insurance companies don't even offer broad form because there are not enough takers on it.

Trapdoors

So now you've picked your policy and added the additional coverage you needed. Done and dusted. All is well. Right?

Well, maybe.

See, there's this nefarious thing in the industry called the "trapdoor." As you'd expect, trapdoors are complicated language embedded in the policy that the insurance companies may lean on to get out of paying claims. Before I go into it any further, I want it to be clear that I disagree with them. In fact I really hate them. Trapdoors are what help give the insurance industry that oily reputation—the used car salesman thing again.

I wish it weren't the case, but you can find insurance policies that are simply loaded with trapdoors. And they are that way by design. We see three hundred to five hundred claims a month, and no matter how hard we try to screen them, there are always a handful of those that don't go as planned, and it breaks my heart a little each time I see it.

The perfect example is the special form policies. You know these are touted as being "all risk" with "limited exclusions," and if they are written the right way, they are.

Unfortunately there are some carriers and some programs out there that say, "Hey, we'll offer special form because we know that everyone wants that. But we really don't want to actually cover everything that special form covers because that could get expensive for us."

On the declarations page of these policies, you'll see in bright letters "special form." But when you dig ninety pages deep into the policy, you'll see language that says you actually have no theft coverage. So unless you read through the endorsement pages thoroughly (and trapdoors are always at the back or in the exclusion pages), you'll never catch them.

So let's say somebody does rip the copper out of your walls, and you think, "It's okay. This is exactly why I decided to pay more for special form coverage." Then you turn in your claim and are shocked when the adjuster calls you and tells you that you don't actually have coverage. "Just look on page ninety of your policy," they say.

And now you are furious because, for one thing, special form *says* it protects against theft, and who on earth is going to read ninety freaking pages of an insurance policy?

Final Thoughts

I don't typically counsel people to choose basic form unless I'm convinced they've got enough money to self-insure. The most positive aspect of the basic form for most investors is pretty obvious: it's cost. The savings can be pretty dramatic when you consider how much 20 to 30 percent per year adds up to.

The next logical step is to think about loss of rents coverage,

> I DON'T TYPICALLY COUNSEL PEOPLE TO CHOOSE BASIC FORM UNLESS I'M CONVINCED THEY'VE GOT ENOUGH MONEY TO SELF-INSURE.

detached structures, and extended coverage if things are blown away or burn to the ground. And if you're in vacation rentals or furnishing your locations, you want some contents coverage (which is called business personal property [BPP]).

From there you have the option to fluff up the form with ancillary products like equipment breakdown, earthquake, flood, or what we call "ordinance and law," which means you can rebuild a home that is destroyed and update it to current codes if it is old. I will go more into this in chapter 8 about coverage gaps, but for now rest assured that options exist for any peril you may worry about.

CHAPTER RECAP

Every investor situation is different, but I think it's safe to say that you all want adequate and appropriate insurance. The first consideration is the type of policy that you want, either basic or special form. A basic form policy covers the basics, including coverage such as fire, wind, hail, and vandalism. The burden of proof for basic form lies with the insured and their agent to prove to the insurance company that the loss that happened was caused by an included peril. Special form covers additional risks, such as water damage, theft, weight of ice, sleet and snow, and collapse, and therefore tends to be a safer option. It is more expensive than basic, which allows for more extensive coverage. Exclusions and trapdoors exist on both forms, and it is a good idea to consider those before choosing a policy.

If you choose to self-insure, meaning you will cover the cost to recover any damages that may take place on your property, you should still get liability coverage.

EXERCISE—CHAPTER 3

Examine your current policy or policies. If you don't have any policies for investment properties at this time, look at your homeowner's policy. Dig through it to find out if you have basic or special (or broad) form and what exclusions are written into it. Read the fine print to see if you can identify any potential trapdoors. Highlight phrases such as the following:

- This Endorsement Changes the Policy; Please Read It Carefully
- Limitation of Coverage
- Policy Amendment
- Exclusion

I encourage you to take these back to your broker or agent to clarify what they really mean in the event of a loss.

CHAPTER 4

HOW CAN I AVOID PAYING TOO MUCH (OR NOT ENOUGH) FOR THE RIGHT COVERAGE?

In the early days of my career, one of my first clients had a property where one of his tenants dropped a lit cigarette on his bed. Instead of taking the time to put the fire out, the tenant freaked out and just ran from the building screaming. His inability to think rationally and simply take a minute to extinguish this slow-burning flame caused $1.2 million of damage to the three-story apartment building.

Fire is one of the worst types of loss in the real estate investing world. I've seen too many properties catch fire due to unattended candles, kitchen mishaps, or tenants deciding to burn their (extremely flammable) Christmas trees for heat in winter.

FIRE IS ONE OF THE WORST TYPES OF LOSS IN THE REAL ESTATE INVESTING WORLD.

Far too often the loss is made worse due to the fact that, like the man who torched his home with a cigarette, the people involved don't do what they should. Homeowners and tenants differ greatly in this respect. Anyone who has been in this game very long will tell you it is not easy to find a tenant who is willing to treat your property with the same care and caution they would if they owned it themselves.

Because of this, when bad things happen, investors really need to know they have the right policies in place. But with that said, depending on how and where you are investing, some coverage options may be overkill.

Let's say you own property in Miami, and you have coverage in your policy for snow. In recorded history it has only snowed once there (for ninety minutes on January 19, 1977, if you're curious), so why are you paying extra money to have coverage that you're never going to use? Of course, snow isn't the only coverage you gain by purchasing special form. All of these additional coverages should be considered before making a decision. As long as you are comfortable with any other exclusions on your policy and have met or exceeded your insurance lending requirements, you shouldn't have to pay for anything you don't feel you need.

But before we get into that, it can be helpful to get a foundation of understanding of how insured values and premiums are determined. The value to which you insure your property usually starts with a price per square foot, either a minimum determined by your carrier or based on an estimated replacement cost to rebuild the home to its current state. Your insurance premium will then be a defined rate per $100 of insured value. So if you have a one-thousand-square-foot home insured at $100 per square foot, you have $100,000 of coverage. Then the rate from the carrier is $0.50 per $100 of coverage. So the way the math is calculated looks like this:

$100,000 / $100 x 0.5 = $500 annual premium for your property coverage

Feel free to substitute your own values to see what your property should be at. The rest of this chapter will help you contemplate your specific needs and examine the policies you currently hold so that you can decide the best and most effective way to continue to insure your investments.

What It Means to Overinsure

Overinsuring a property means exactly what you think it does: insuring it for more than its actual value. If the property is worth $300,000 and you're insuring it for $500,000, you're overinsured. This may seem like a no-brainer, right? Who is going to be stupid enough to insure their property for more than it is actually worth? Well, it's a lot more common than you think.

Here's how it happens: Let's say you're thinking about purchasing 123 Main Street, and you're shopping for insurance ahead of time. You contact an agent with the details, and they do some research. They run their rebuilding cost estimator, and based on market conditions and labor costs, they come back to you and say, "This is what you need to insure the property for."

Sometimes that's such an inflated number (often between $150 and $600 per square foot or higher, depending on where you are in the country) that it almost encourages you to burn the property down for profit. It doesn't make any sense. But because we tend to trust those who are more "expert" than us, we just go with it and try not to think too much about the money we are spending on something we might never ever need.

I have known people to purchase properties in certain parts of the country for $5,000 apiece with a plan to flip them. They go to a traditional insurance agent and are told that they have to insure their purchase for $80,000–$90,000. And then they come to me and ask why. Of course a lot of this is market driven, but that seems pretty high no matter where you are. I do my best to explain how their agent came up with this number, and then I review the options they have available. In fact this is a big part of why I wrote this book—to basically share with you the same thing I share with them.

Now before you jump to the conclusion that you should always choose the lowest amount possible, there are advantages to increasing that insured value. In many instances you might as well self-insure if you can. But be careful that your $5,000 investment property doesn't become a $10,000 headache when there is a fire or a flood. This is an instance when you would be underinsured.

There is certainly a happy medium.

Note that if you invest in one of the twenty "valued policy" states in America, the rules are different than other states. In these states if the insurance company decides that they'll insure the property for $1 million and the property burns to the ground, then no questions are asked, and you're paid $1 million. It's common in these valued policy states that insurance companies are stricter on how high a value

YOU NEVER INSURE FOR LAND VALUE ON YOUR PROPERTY COVERAGE.

per square foot they'll insure a property for. They want to be certain they are not overpaying on a total loss because land value was factored in the insured value. In some states (think California), the land value can be worth more than the structure itself and is often included in the calculations of the insured value—especially when there is a lender involved.

When there is a question on the accuracy of the insured value being requested for a property, the insurance company may require a property appraisal to approve the limit of coverage requested.

Here's a quick tip: you never insure for land value on your property coverage. Think about it. If the property burns to the ground, the land is still there for you to rebuild on or sell.

Each valued policy state applies the law uniquely, as you can see in the following table.

Table 1. https://www.iamagazine.com/strategies/read/2018/01/09/ what-you-need-to-know-about-valued-policy-states

AR	All real property	Fire and natural disasters (excluding flood and quake)
CA	Buildings	All perils covered by the property policy
FL	Any building (incl. mobile & manufactured homes)	All perils covered by the property policy
GA	One- or two-family residential buildings	Fire
KS	All improvements on real property	Fire, tornado, wind, lightning
LA	Inanimate or immovable property	Fire
MN	All property	All perils covered by the policy
MS	Buildings	Fire
MO	All property	Fire
MT	Improvements to real property	All perils covered by the property policy
NE	Real property	Fire, tornado, wind, lightning, explosion
NH	Buildings	Fire and lightning
ND	Real property	All perils covered by the property policy
OH	Any building	Fire and lightning
SC	All real property	Fire
SD	Real property	Fire, lightning, and tornado
TN	Any building	Fire
TX	All real property	Fire
WV	Real property	All perils covered by the property policy
WI	Owner-occupied dwellings	All perils covered by the property policy

There is power in knowing what the conditions are in the areas you invest in. I know one property manager who handles hundreds of locations, including multifamily and single-family units. He's the best example of what it means to be a good steward. He has investor clients who come from all around the world. He sits down and talks them through the reality of the markets they invest in and advises them on how they should insure their property based on his real-world experience and knowledge. I wish every investor who worked with a property manager was as fortunate. Most investors have to rely on the advice of their agents, and, unfortunately, that advice may or may not be the best suited for your specific circumstance.

You might be wondering why any reasonable agent would ever recommend overinsuring. One reason is economics. Some of the big national carriers tend to be reluctant about offering coverage on investment properties. They do it almost out of a sense of obligation to their existing client base, but they don't make that service well known. These companies specialize in home, auto, and life, and each agency probably has only a handful of real estate investors within every agent's book of business. This means they're not actively pursuing insurance opportunities for those investor clients. These clients are not as lucrative as those in the other parts of the agency, so to make a profit, they substantially overinsure those investment properties. The agent will give the investment property a much higher valuation per square foot, which leads to a higher total insured value, which increases the premium cost. This makes it worth their time.

Another reason agents might overinsure is simply because they don't understand the way these types of policies work. They don't understand the risk that goes into them or the way that these properties are settled on claims. Things of that nature are very different from a homeowner's policy. Often, these investors will look at these properties and say, "Yeah, I don't want to insure it for $200 a square foot. Hell, if the thing burns to the ground, I'm not going to rebuild it anyway. So let me save on insurance and insure to a more adequate value that I feel as an investor is appropriate for my risk that I'm taking on." Inexperienced agents will balk at the thought.

And so do carriers. Often they flat-out refuse to offer any flexibility for these clients at all. They come back to the investor and say, "Nope, it doesn't matter. It's a thousand-square-foot home, and you're going to insure it for $250,000. End of story."

Then if you have a loss, unless it's a total loss and you're in a valued policy state, you're not going to recover that $250,000. So you're overinsuring—you're paying more for your coverage with little to no ability to recover all that money.

In the end it's about doing the right thing for you and for your business and knowing whom to trust when people are giving you advice.

I do the exact opposite. I negotiate my policies with the carriers that power my program for some benchmarks, and then I rely on the investor client. Often, my clients are contractors with work crews who can get losses repaired for significantly less than what an insurance carrier thinks they can because they don't have a grip on the market or how much it's going to cost. I let the investor tell me what amount they feel is adequate to insure their property, so that a) it's a reasonable price and b) it's a comfortable insured value that the investor knows. That way if they happen to suffer a partial or total loss, they'll be made whole based on their needs.

Insurance companies rarely notice the benefit of allowing an investor to insure to a lower insured value. It limits their exposure following a total loss. On the thousand-square-foot home just used in the prior example, if it burns to the ground, and it's insured to $100K and not $250K, it just saved the carrier $150K.

Actual Cash Value Coverage (ACV) and Replacement Cost Coverage (RC)

As your portfolio grows, insurance may seem like a creative way to save some money on your property expenses, but you want to save money the right way. Knowing the difference between "actual cash value" and "replacement cost" is very important, particularly if you are a new investor. At first glance these terms might appear to be highly complicated and thereby not worth the struggle to figure out, but this is one instance where the old saying "knowledge is power" is really true. It can make a huge difference in feeling confident you have the right amount of coverage.

Most investors have, unfortunately, lived through a property loss, like what we described. God bless you if you haven't yet! But at one point or another, if you're investing in real estate, you're going to experience something similar to what I just talked about. And when it does, you will find yourself with the same concerns clients bring to us on a daily basis: "Why can't I recover my deductible? Why do I have to prove that I paid additional money? Why the hell am I paying all this money for my insurance when they're going to give me a fraction of what they said I would get?"

I confess this section is one of the main reasons I wrote this book. Investors like you come from all walks of life—from the sweet grandma who just retired and thinks real estate investing might be a fun thing to try to professional contractors with a whole slew of builders. One of the most common and most difficult conversations we have is with those families who just inherited a house from someone who passed away. And they come to us asking, "What are we going to do with it? We don't want to sell it. Do we want to make it an investment property and rent it out? What do we need to know? Can we just keep Grandma's homeowner's policy in place?"

No. Absolutely not. (More about that later.)

"Then what is the best policy to get?"

A big part of that decision is whether you check the box marked ACV or the box marked RC.

DEFINITIONS

Actual cash value (ACV) coverage is an option that you can choose on your insurance policy that gives you cash for the *actual* value of the loss, just like the name says. Claim settlements are calculated with deductions for depreciation considerations like age, condition, and useful life expectancy. In return for allowing you to insure your property for a lower insured value per square foot, the insurance companies limit you to one settlement payment following a property claim after factoring in this actual value estimation that is recommended by the adjuster and approved by the carrier.

CONSIDER WHAT YOU WOULD DO IF YOU HAD A TOTAL LOSS AT ONE OF YOUR PROPERTIES.

Replacement cost (RC) coverage, by definition, simply provides you with the ability to go back and recover any depreciation initially taken from you in the claims process, but in order to garner this additional payout, you have to insure your property to a higher value per square foot. RC coverage can be obtained by insuring locations to $80 per square foot or more in our program. Every insurance carrier has a different threshold at which you can garner replacement cost coverage, and most are significantly higher than $80. This value is not a guarantee and should not be confused with the reconstruction cost of the property.

Here's a quick tip: consider what you would do if you had a total loss at one of your properties. If you know that you would not rebuild, then ACV may be an option you want to consider. If you would rebuild, it might make sense to go with RC. The only exception to this is if there is a loan on the property. Many lenders require RC regardless. The cost difference between ACV and RC is about 20 to 25 percent, in most cases.

Loss Settlement That Doesn't Match Your Investment Strategy

Let's talk through a few scenarios to put this in context. Say you have a kitchen fire, which is a partial loss and is the most common thing that we see in our program. Your tenant left a burner on and left the room. They catch it before it spreads to other rooms, but the kitchen is pretty much destroyed.

The insurance company comes to you to adjust the claim, and they say it would cost $30,000 to rebuild your kitchen the way it was. With ACV, they will depreciate everything that was damaged, including the appliances, the flooring, the cabinets—everything. Each of these depreciates at a different level, but on average it's about 1 percent per year off. They will start with the last time the kitchen was replaced or renovated, not the original year it was built. The industry average for depreciation is about 20 to 22 percent.

So let's just say for nice round numbers they say they are going to depreciate it at 20 percent. The deduction is $6,000, which leaves the payment at $24,000.

Then what do they do? They look at your deductible, right? Because that's the amount that you agreed to self-insure. This is a good reason not to overstretch yourself, but also don't carry a deductible so low that you're overpaying for your insurance. It's kind of a game you have to play a little bit. Everybody's answer is different.

So let's just say you have a $5,000 deductible to make it a nice round number. In this example, it would leave you with $19,000 cash, actual cash value settlement, to cover that $30,000 kitchen.

That's all you can recover. But in reality that is usually more than enough to make you whole again, particularly if you've got your own crews or you're completing the work yourself. You know the difference between paying retail for labor and materials and doing it for a fraction of the price. For most real estate investors, they would look at that burned-out kitchen and think, "No way is this going to cost me thirty grand. I'll do it for half that."

If this sounds like you, ACV might be a good option for you to consider.

The difference with RC is that it provides you with the ability to recover the depreciation that was initially levied against you during the claims process, but insurance companies require a couple of things from you. They do make it difficult on you. The first thing they do is give you the actual cash value settlement. So in this example, we start with the same $19,000 after depreciation and deductible. They give you that check right away and set you loose to fix it yourself.

They require you to exhaust the $19,000 on your repairs. If there are outstanding repairs that remain, you make those remaining repairs out of pocket, and then you submit the receipts to your insurance carrier, and they'll reimburse you for up to what the original undepreciated amount was up to $6,000. The only part that is not recoverable on the RC policy is your deductible.

But you actually have to prove to them exactly what the out-of-pocket costs were to make you whole again. It may go without saying, but you have to replace like with like. I can't take linoleum and replace it with marble. They're going to raise an eyebrow if you try to fit upgrades in and claim them as part of the repairs.

But all of this is to reinforce the importance of knowing your exit strategy and knowing your resources. Are you flipping or holding? Do you have crews who get things done for cheaper than retail costs? Or are you new to investing and need to be cautious about placing additional financial hardship on yourself?

If you own the property outright or don't have much left on your loan, you can often negotiate with your lender to consider allowing you to carry ACV and save yourself 20 or 25 percent.

Here's something else to consider. Let's say you buy a ten-year-old apartment complex in western Kansas. As you review your insurance policy options, you notice that even though you have a replacement cost property policy, there may be an ACV endorsement tied to roof damage. Now let's say a tornado hits the complex and blows off the roof. You think, "Good thing I have replacement cost coverage. I'll get more than enough money to replace that roof."

But then you dig a hundred pages deep into your policy, and it says your roof is limited to ACV from day one, regardless of the policy that you chose and age of your roof. This means you'll only get what the insurance company decides is the actual value of that roof after its depreciation has been figured in.

Side note: Once the roof passes a certain age—five, seven and a half, ten, twelve, or fifteen years old, depending on the carrier—it's limited to the actual *useful life that is left*, even if you purchased a replacement cost policy. If your property is a decade old, according to some policies, there's little to no useful life left. Be sure to review which ACV roof endorsement is present on your property policy with your agent.

It is really important to read your policy ahead of time, and if there are things you don't understand or don't want, challenge your agent. Make sure that they're disclosing everything to you. Remember that your investment strategy is key to making the best decision for your portfolio. If you suffer a loss, how quickly and cost effectively can you rebuild?

But take note: total losses are a little bit different. If the property completely burns to the ground or blows away, you don't have to worry about depreciation or deductible. None of that matters. You get paid what's on the declarations page of your policy in most instances. Of course, total losses are extremely rare.

Something to keep in mind is that, of all my clients who are insured with RC policies, when they suffer a partial loss similar to the first example, around 65 percent of them never come back to recover the depreciation. It's not because they don't want to. It's because the actual cash value settlement that was provided to them by the insurance company was more than enough to make them whole again. They can work faster and cheaper than big-name carriers every day.

But even if you are a seasoned investor with crews at the ready, you might decide to carry RC because the property is in a great neighborhood with a waiting list to fill, and if there were a loss, you'd want to rebuild ASAP so that you don't lose any cash flow. You don't want any hiccups, and it's better safe than sorry. That's a good option for you.

Talk to your agent or your client service representative about this, and really determine the right type of coverage for your particular investment property portfolio. Don't let insurance break the bank. Even though you only have two options here, there are layers of decision making. Every carrier is different, and you need to know your goals. Are you concerned about total loss more than partial loss? Are you concerned that you can't pay out of pocket? Are there other factors that might influence that decision, like the current market conditions or the level of luxury you have at your property? What is the size of your portfolio? What is your loss history?

Why So Many Get It Wrong

Why do so many household-name insurance companies screw up this conversation? Well, think about it. They offer very little by way of options because they are focused on doing what's best for the general body of their clients. They are phenomenal at what they do because they are focused on their part of the industry. They do homeowners really well. They do auto very well. But when you look at an investment property, they often don't know what the heck to do with it. It's no different than if you asked me to insure your personal autos or sell you life insurance—it's not my specialty, and I'm not the ideal agent for you to work with.

> OF ALL MY CLIENTS INSURED WITH RC POLICIES, AROUND 65 PERCENT NEVER COME BACK TO RECOVER THE DEPRECIATION.

Most of these big companies don't have a very high appetite for these types of risks, and they aren't necessarily nimble enough to customize based on individual needs. There are limitations to the coverage that aren't favorable to an investor. As you become a professional investor and you start to grow in your portfolio, you might start to feel that the big companies want nothing to do with you.

There is a disadvantage to working with the largest, household-name companies in that when you go to them, you are working with a "captive agent." These are people who can only offer the policies that their single company has to offer. Most of the time, these agents don't have the ability to go out and shop that risk around for their clients. They offer one product, take it or leave it.

If you work with an independent agent who has access to multiple companies, you'll find more flexibility.

So instead of a single option with a captive agent, independent agents will come back to you with multiple options that are competitive both in terms of coverages and costs. And you're going to have advantages and disadvantages to each, which any good agent can walk you through.

You have to understand that you are a risk to the insurance companies. Non-owner-occupied dwellings, renovation locations, and certainly vacant locations are considered higher risk. Investing in Montana is different from Florida or Michigan, so there is no single one-size-fits-all coverage option that works best.

But no matter where you are located or the type of portfolio you have, you can avoid overpaying for coverage and still have the ability to be made whole following a loss.

You can control the costs of your insurance by finding a coverage package that's unique to you and your investing strategy.

The key to finding that best coverage package is by first determining your property valuation and your business goals. Some people might not consider paying more for their coverage to be overpaying, but they pay more to make themselves feel better. Others don't want to pay a penny over what is required legally and ethically.

It's about finding the right niche products for what you're doing. You need to work with specialists who do nothing but this because they'll have an appetite for this kind of business. They offer policies built specifically for revenue-generating assets (or at least what are supposed to be once they become occupied).

The Solution

There are steps you can take to avoid overinsuring your property without risking adequate coverage. The first is to do your due diligence. Find out what claims have been made against the property in the past. You can get a loss run report by requesting the seller obtain it from their insurance agent. This report provides a detailed summary of the losses suffered at the property (both property and liability) during the time the seller owned the location. This will tell you if the location is prone to flooding or has a tenant who may be problematic for you.

If you're purchasing your property from a homeowner, you'll want to obtain a comprehensive loss underwriting exchange (CLUE) report. This report provides details on the losses that occurred at the property during the seller's time owning the property. You'll read more about the CLUE report in chapter 5, so feel free to tuck any questions away for a minute.

If you're familiar with George Orwell's book *1984,* you might see a comparison with insurance companies and Big Brother in that they all share information about losses with data companies like LexisNexis, which makes that data accessible to every other insurance company.

The last thing you want is for the insurance company to come to you and say, "You didn't let us know that there have been three different fire claims over the last twelve months. We agreed to charge you $500 a year for your annual insurance premium. After learning of these past losses, we're instead going to charge you $2,700 a year to ensure we are collecting adequate premium to offset the higher risk." Or "We're going to cancel your policy altogether because we don't like the risk."

I can tell you that 70 percent of the property claims we see outside of hurricanes and wildfires are tenant-caused negligent losses. These are the living room fires from a candle left burning or kitchen fires. You want access to carriers that understand this risk and specialize in it. That's why it's so important to partner with the right retail agent who has

DO YOU REALLY KNOW WHAT IT IS YOU'RE PAYING FOR?

those relationships already established. Even if it's just a handful of carriers, that's better than one or two. Ideally you go to your agent at any time, and they would be able to tell you all the options available out there. And then they could say, "By the way, here are the advantages of option A, and here are the disadvantages. B is better in this way, and here's where C is better."

They have their finger on the pulse of the industry that well.

Preferably your agent will have an interest in real estate investing themselves. They don't have to be an investor. Maybe they're just a part of a real estate investor association, but it cuts down on the back and forth and the chances that something gets lost in the shuffle if you're both speaking the same language.

Another step you can take is to actually read your policy. This may seem like a no-brainer, but so many people neglect to do this. Do you *really* know what it is you're paying for? Back to the snow in Miami, are you paying extra money to have that coverage that you're never going to use? Know exactly what your insurance lending requirements are, and once you have met those, consider if you really want to exceed them too.

CHAPTER RECAP

Finding the right balance between being over- and underinsured might feel a bit like walking a tightrope. There are risks to both. Nobody wants to pay too much money for not-enough insurance. That kind of unrecoverable loss is frustrating at best. Most people also don't want to risk not having enough coverage for potential risks and ending up having to pay out of pocket after a loss. Knowing the conditions in the areas you invest can offer an advantage.

Also, understanding how insurance policies use actual cash value coverage versus replacement cost coverage will offer insight into how your policy will function if put into use. Remember: actual cash value (ACV) coverage gives you cash for the *actual* value of the loss. Replacement cost (RC) coverage provides you with the ability to go back and recover any depreciation initially taken from you in the claims process. Clearly articulating your investment strategy can help bring clarity to this decision.

EXERCISE–CHAPTER 4

Consider an investment property in your portfolio. Choose one property and determine which loss settlement method is best for you.

Imagine a kitchen fire at that property that the adjuster determines to be a $25,000 loss.

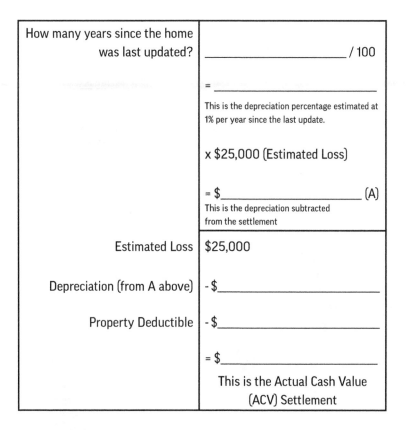

How many years since the home was last updated?	_____ / 100
	= _____
	This is the depreciation percentage estimated at 1% per year since the last update.
	x $25,000 (Estimated Loss)
	= $_____ (A) This is the depreciation subtracted from the settlement
Estimated Loss	$25,000
Depreciation (from A above)	- $_____
Property Deductible	- $_____
	= $_____
	This is the Actual Cash Value (ACV) Settlement

Would this actual cash value settlement be enough to make you whole again in consideration of your business goals?

If not, refer back to the depreciation amount to determine if the amount deducted would be needed to make you whole. In that case you may want to choose replacement cost.

IN CASE YOU ARE WONDERING: CAN COINSURANCE HARM YOU?

By definition, coinsurance is an industry-wide property insurance provision that states the amount of coverage that must be maintained, as a percentage of the total value of the property at the time of loss (as determined by your insurance company), for the insured to collect the full amount of a loss. In other words …

Coinsurance is a term that seems harmless enough. There must be something good about it if it exists, right? Okay, I'll give you that. There is something good. One thing: having a coinsurance percentage on your policy can reduce the premium you pay significantly.

There you have it.

But what are you not being told?

The Risks of Coinsurance

Coinsurance is a creative way insurance companies can greatly diminish the amount of money you recover following a loss. They do this by determining you are not insured adequately to value at the time of loss.

Common coinsurance requirements are between 80 to 100 percent of the calculated reconstruction cost of the property at the time of loss. The higher the coinsurance percentage is on the policy, the worse it will be for you.

That's the X factor because you'll never know what the actual true replacement cost of the property is until the loss actually happens, and it can fluctuate a lot.

Let's assume you suffered a partial property loss at one of your locations. Following the loss, your insurance company will come to you and say, "If the property had burned to the ground, it would cost $100,000 to rebuild it. You've got an 80 percent coinsurance clause on the property, so as long as you're insured on the declarations page to $80,000 or higher, then you've met your coinsurance clause, and we will not assess any coinsurance penalty against the settlement amount." If, however, you're underinsured (maybe you insured that property for $60,000), you're going to get hit pretty substantially on a coinsurance penalty that decreases the amount of money you can recover following that loss.

Often, this is coming from the same carriers and agents who don't give any guidance on what you should insure that property for in the first place. Some of these carriers are fine to insure a property to thirty or forty bucks a square foot because they know they're going to get a hefty coinsurance penalty put into that loss settlement and pay pennies on the dollar on that loss.

Gives Insurance Companies a Way Out

There are a lot of carriers in our space that do this, but if you're ever tempted to get into a coinsurance agreement, don't. It has little to no benefit to the investor. In fact you can get dinged pretty badly on a property loss if you're insured this way. If I'm not being clear enough about how I feel on this topic, not a single one of our program's contracts has coinsurance.

Personally I don't want that reputation. I don't want my investors having that fight after a loss. And I don't want to fight that fight. As you know by now, because these properties are non-owner-occupied dwellings or vacant or undergoing renovations, they are considered higher risk by the insurance industry as a whole. A lot of carriers will try to put as many safety nets into their coverage as they can in order to minimize their exposure.

I know that this can be used as a creative way for insurance companies to diminish the amount of money that an investor gets post loss, despite the fact they're collecting adequate premium to offset the risk—which we have to assume is true, considering they set the premiums they charge. I don't want

> **IF YOU'RE EVER TEMPTED TO GET INTO A COINSURANCE AGREEMENT, DON'T.**

to make it seem like I don't appreciate insurance companies, but when it comes to coinsurance, I have very little patience. There's no reason you should have to get dinged for some magical term within an insurance policy that few understand.

Diminishes the Money You Can Recover Following a Loss

Here's a quick example: One of your investment properties is insured to $100,000 and suffers hail damage. The coverage you have is ACV (see chapter 4), and you have an 80 percent coinsurance clause in your policy. The adjuster who is assigned to your case comes up with an adjusted amount for that loss in the amount of $25,000. For this example, we will assume that the depreciation percentage from each situation is 20 percent, and your wind deductible is $5,000.

At the time of the loss, the adjuster determines the reconstruction value of the property to be $235,000. Per your 80 percent coinsurance clause, you have agreed to be insured to at least $188,000 (which is the $235,000 times that 80 percent clause).

The carrier will divide your $100,000 of coverage into $188,000 and determine that you are 46.8 percent underinsured, and you will be slapped with a hefty coinsurance penalty deduction before the depreciation deductible. If your declarations page had shown $188,000, you'd have been okay. But it didn't. Too bad.

Then comes the depreciation reduction. Across the entire scope of the loss, this is calculated by year built and update records such as HVAC, plumbing, roof, etc., for everything that was damaged by the hailstorm. Just as a rule of thumb, everything depreciates at a different level—roughly 1 percent per year from last update, with the exception being the roof (see chapter 4), which depreciates at an accelerated rate due to the constant exposure to weather.

And finally, the deductible is taken from what's left.

Broken down, it looks like this:

- Amount of loss—$25,000
- Coinsurance penalty—$11,700
- Depreciation amount—$5,000
- Wind deductible—$5,000

For a total adjusted settlement of $3,300.

That's a long way from the $25,000 that you need to repair that hail damage.

To give coinsurance more perspective, here's a comparison of what a claim looks like with and without it.

The home in question suffered a near total loss estimated at $100,000. The true replacement cost at the time of partial loss was determined to be $230,000. The home was insured to $125,000 with a $10,000 deductible on an ACV. Let's look at what happens with and without an 80 percent coinsurance clause.

	80% COINSURANCE	NO COINSURANCE
AMOUNT POSSIBLE TO RECOVER FOLLOWING THE LOSS	$100,000	$100,000
COINSURANCE PENALTY	$32,000	$0
20 PERCENT DEPRECIATION	$20,000	$20,000
DEDUCTIBLE	$10,000	$10,000
TOTAL ADJUSTED SETTLEMENT	$38,000	$70,000

As you see, that coinsurance penalty can significantly diminish the amount of money you are able to recover following a loss.

Guessing Game on True Replacement Cost

Knowing the true replacement cost (see chapter 4) of a given property ahead of time is tricky. Replacement/rebuilding costs fluctuate so frequently that until the loss actually occurs, the true replacement/rebuild cost is somewhat of a mystery. Below are some factors that can contribute:

1. Catastrophic event: Think hurricane, superstorm, or wildfire. These events drive labor and material costs soaring because of the immediate rise in demand.
2. Inflation: As I write this book, we are in the midst of such an event. Costs for lumber, concrete, gasoline, and other commodities are through the roof.
3. Labor shortage: Again, something we are living through as I write this. The demand for quality, skilled labor is up, and that drives pricing up.

How can you know what it's going to take to repair a property in the next year? Five years? Ten?

The answer? You can't. And neither can the insurance companies.

Coinsurance in the Real World

I've seen a lot of investors harmed by this. They'll come to me and say, "Shawn, what the heck just happened?"

And then I show them the coinsurance provision and what it would have been without that provision. It's night and day, which is another reason I encourage you to challenge your agent. If you see anything about coinsurance on your policy, go back right away, and tell them to remove it. Typically you can do so by paying a little bit of additional premium. It may be a couple hundred dollars a year, depending on the carrier. It could be more than that. Companies can be all over the place on this. But if it's on there, get rid of it.

If you're with a carrier that simply won't remove it, then you're with a carrier that doesn't have the appetite for your needs, and you probably need to start shopping around.

Exercise—Mini Section

- Go to the declarations page of your property policy and see if there is a coinsurance percentage.
- If there is, ask your agent to run a replacement cost estimation and confirm in writing that you will meet your coinsurance clause without penalty if your property were to suffer a loss today.
- If your agent is unwilling to confirm this and the RC estimator shows you are not insured to at least your coinsurance percentage, then request that your agent remove the coinsurance clause. If they are unable to, then you should increase your insured value to meet the coinsurance requirements.

COMMERCIAL PROPERTY COVERAGE PART DECLARATIONS

**WOEDL
INSURANCE
COMPANY**

1. POLICY NO. WIC52680

EFFECTIVE DATE 6/30/2022

2. NAMED INSURED Josephine Investor

RENEWAL OF WIC52679

3. DESCRIPTION OF PREMISES ☐"X" If supplemental declarations attached

Prem. No.	Bldg. No.	Location, Construction and Occupancy
		Various - As per Schedule submitted to the Company on 6/17/2022

COVERAGES PROVIDED – Insurance at the described premises applies only for coverages for which a limit of insurance is shown.

Prem. No.	Bldg. No.	Coverage	Limit of Insurance	Covered Causes of Loss	Coinsurance*	Rates
All	All	Building, Business Income with Extra Expense including "Rental Value"	$ 18,973,671 Subject to conditions of the Scheduled Limit of Liability.	Special	Nil	Included

*IF EXTRA EXPENSE COVERAGE, LIMITS ON LOSS PAYMENT

OPTIONAL COVERAGES – Applicable only when entries are made in the schedule below.

Prem. No.	Bldg. No.	Agreed Value Expiration Date	Coverage	Amount	Replacement Cost (X) Building	Personal Property	Including "Stock"
All	All				X**		

Prem. No.	Bldg. No.	Inflation Guard (Percentage) Building	Personal Property	* Monthly Limit of Indemnity (Fraction)	* Maximum Period of Indemnity (X)	* Extended Period of Indemnity (Days)
N/A						

* APPLIES TO BUSINESS INCOME ONLY

4. MORTGAGE HOLDERS AND/OR LOSS PAYEES

Prem. No.	Bldg. No.	Mortgage Holder and/or Loss Payee Name and Mailing Address
		N/A

5. DEDUCTIBLE

Please refer to the Deductible & Period of Restoration Endorsement

**TOTAL PREMIUM
FOR THIS ⇨ $ INCLUDED
COVERAGE PART**

6. FORMS / ENDORSEMENTS APPLICABLE

SEE SCHEDULE OF POLICY ATTACHMENTS AND FORMS, WIC 98135 101

THESE DECLARATIONS, WHEN COMBINED WITH THE COMMON POLICY DECLARATIONS, THE COMMON POLICY CONDITIONS, COVERAGE FORM(S) AND ENDORSEMENTS, IF ANY, ISSUED TO FORM A PART THEREOF, COMPLETE THE CONTRACT OF INSURANCE.

Includes copyrighted material of ISO Commercial Risk Services, Inc., with its permission.
Copyright. ISO Commercial Risk Services, Inc., 1984.

WIC 11142022

CHAPTER 5

WHAT IS THE RIGHT PROPERTY DEDUCTIBLE FOR ME?

Too many investors view insurance as a maintenance plan as opposed to a way to help manage sudden and unforeseen damage, which is the primary purpose of insurance, leading many to turn in claims for things that they shouldn't. And in turn, this causes insurance companies to raise their rates for everyone (regardless of their individual loss history) to remain profitable.

How Deductibles Work

This chapter focuses on property deductible structures and how to use them to your advantage. This is an area where I do things differently than the rest of the industry. You could come to me and say, "Hey, Shawn, I need to insure 123 Main Street because I'm buying it, and I'm going to put a tenant in there."

Most agents will send you back a quote that says, "Here's the cost of your premium, and it's a $500 property deductible."

Often people just accept that at face value and move on. But you, as the investor, need to understand that the more creative you can get with your deductible structures, the better it is for you. The insurance company sets that lower deductible because it means they collect more premium dollars. They're banking on the loss not happening. But in your case, that's not usually in your best interest.

The average property deductible we see in our program is around $2,500–$5,000 per insured location. This amount allows the client to keep their payment lower and for our program to provide fair, consistent rates across the board. If your insurance company won't give you credit for a higher deductible, it's time to start shopping for a new one.

I always encourage my investors to think about the minimum loss they simply could not fix out of pocket because it would harm their business financially, and that's where we start when considering their property deductible. Some investors will do as much as double that amount because the higher the property deductible, the lower the property rate.

CHOOSE A PROPERTY DEDUCTIBLE AMOUNT THAT YOU'RE OKAY SELF-INSURING.

Choose a property deductible amount that you're okay self-insuring, meaning you can pay for it yourself without harming your business or your livelihood.

Your deductible is the amount you are responsible for in the event of a property loss before your insurance company starts to pay a claim. The higher the deductible, the lower your cost. The amount includes your assigned all other perils (AOP) property deductible, which doesn't typically include wind/hail or named windstorm and sometimes doesn't include water damage or theft and vandalism/ malicious mischief either. Insurance companies will carve these perils out of the policy and assign higher deductibles. Provided you're okay with this, it can save you money and still meet your lending institution's insurance guidelines. The required deductible listed in their guidelines typically only pertains to your AOP deductible. Some may also have a separate requirement for wind, hail, and named windstorm as well.

What you really need to know is that the deductible you carry on your policy will directly affect your monthly (and annual) premium amount assigned to you by the carrier.

The fact that you have a say in your deductible might come as a surprise to you. Most insurance companies don't allow their clients to tinker much with deductible amounts because there have been scams that abused the system. It's the same reason insurance costs are continuing to go up and are skyrocketing for investors.

If I'm carrying a $5,000 deductible and my property gets $2,000 worth of damage, then I'll have to pay for those repairs out of pocket because insurance won't pay out until damage exceeds my deductible. I'd be foolish to turn that claim in to my insurance company because they're going to say, "This doesn't exceed your deductible, so you're on your own." But I'm okay because I have been saving every month with a lower premium, and I was smart enough to put that savings away in the event of a loss—that is, if I have actually been saving money every month. If that $2,000 is going to break me financially, then my deductible was too high.

The Sweet Spot

There is a sweet spot that everyone can find when it comes to balancing the expense of insurance with the most appropriate level of risk. Where people often miss the mark is when they don't know what questions to ask. Investors who are trying real estate out for the first time often decide they want to try flipping just to see how it works out. But because they have never dabbled in this market before, they don't know that there are options.

They know that they need insurance because the mortgage company told them they do, but they don't want to pay too much. This is common with larger homes, like a $250,000–$300,000 house where their premiums are a surprise monthly expense. This is usually a lot more than normal investors realize when they are first getting started. One way you offset that cost is to consider deductible options.

I had a client who fell into this category. He was new to real estate investing and was trying to make the best decisions he could. I sat down with him and presented deductible amounts of $2,500, $5,000, and $10,000. After asking me a lot of questions and weighing his options, he chose to go with $10,000 (despite my recommendation to start with a lower deductible) because the property was vacant at the time, and he didn't feel there was much risk.

Not much time passed before his property suffered a fire loss that caused significant damage but not a total loss. He was awarded a $30,000 settlement to recover the loss, but after the depreciation was assessed and he had to pay that hefty deductible, he walked away with just $15,000. He did not have a crew or any resources like a professional investor might have at his disposal. That was sad to see. He recovered, but it was a lot harder on him than it would have been if he had chosen a lower deductible.

If you're a newbie investor, and you're trying to cut corners, take some time to consider what you will do if something similar happens to you. Do you have your own contractors? Can you do the work yourself? What exactly would it take for you to recover from a loss and still make money on your investment?

Think about that question and write down a number. That's pretty much what you should start with when you consider your deductible. Some investors will as much as double that.

So if you think that any loss under $5,000 is something you easily will pay out of pocket, then that's where you should start. But then if anything over that $5,000 is going to really destroy you, you should take that into account and request a lower deductible.

The deductible is there for a reason, which is for you to have some skin in the game and to show the insurance company that you're involved in the business and that you want to share in the risk. It also hints that you aren't going to ruin your own business for the insurance money.

The deductible conversation is one that you need to have with your agent every year. A lot can happen in twelve months, you know. Maybe you buy ten more properties that are all cash flowing and find yourself in a much better position than before. Maybe you want to save money on insurance premiums now that you are more seasoned with fixing things and have a network of contractors built up.

Sometimes investors come to me at this annual check-in and say, "Shawn, I've been paying insurance premiums for ten years, and I've never had a property loss. I can't help but think about all that money I paid into insurance that I didn't end up needing because I never made a claim. I could have bought five more properties with what I spent. I'm thinking of pulling the plug on the whole thing."

To which I respond, "Why don't we look at increasing your deductible instead of just removing your property coverage altogether? Let's entertain increasing your property deductible from $5,000 to $10,000 or even $25,000 and see what that cost looks like."

I know I have said this before, but I'll say it again—insurance is not one size fits all. It all goes back to investors having choices. If your agent is not telling you that or giving you options, you're with the wrong agent and the wrong insurance company. Bottom line: you deserve to have choices that best fit your investing goals.

Review your existing declarations pages. If your deductible is lower than you would ever file a claim for, you are paying the insurance company more than you need to. Go back to your agent, and tell them to raise your property deductible in an effort to decrease your annual cost. If they can't accommodate this request, you might have the wrong agent.

In the end you can find that sweet spot that will match your goals and your budget.

Factors That Can Influence Your Choice

PERSONAL FINANCES/LIQUIDITY

I have covered this aspect above, but as an investor, this tends to be the first and most important factor when determining your deductible.

If you are running your investments like a business, you know your liquidity, and you know exactly what you can handle in terms of sudden and unforeseen expenses. When it comes to deductibles, it's really being able to answer questions such as "Am I comfortable? Can I sleep at night knowing the risks of my portfolio? Am I overextended? Am I leaving money on the table?"

LOSS HISTORY AND PREVIOUS CLAIMS

This is where you have to do your due diligence prior to purchase. Knowing the risk you are getting into with a new property can be very helpful prior to purchasing and insuring that property. Maybe the property is in a high-hazard wind or hail zone. Maybe there has been a record of vandalism every time the property is vacant.

How do you know this? By using the information available in two reports: the CLUE report or the loss run report.

> **USE THE INFORMATION AVAILABLE IN THE CLUE REPORT OR THE LOSS RUN REPORT.**

CLUE Report

A comprehensive loss underwriting exchange (CLUE) report is a matter of public record and includes any insurance claims made by a policyholder on a home. (Fun fact: there are CLUE reports for vehicles too, if you're looking to buy a used car.)

Under the federal Fair Credit Reporting Act, anyone can pay a small fee to request a copy of a CLUE report on any potential new property by visiting LexisNexis or a similar data company. You can also request it from the seller. The report generally includes the date of claims in the last five to seven years, the type of claim that was made, how much was paid out, and any other relevant details.

Having this report before you buy insurance can help you anticipate what you will need to have based on the history of that property. It can also help shed light on possible hidden damage from past problems. Watch for claims with large payouts and/or high frequency, as those can also be red flags. Frequency can be just as bad as severity. A trend of frequent claims with low payouts can be a sign of things to come. This is especially true in terms of liability coverage, which we will get to in the next chapter.

Look for good news as well. If the claim was paid out for a new roof or windows, you can factor that into your depreciation figures.

If a CLUE report is blank, this could mean that the homeowner didn't make any insurance claims for a while, there were unreported incidents, or they used a company that does not report its claims to LexisNexis. It's not required by law.

Interesting side note while I'm on this topic: Insurance companies use these reports constantly in determining rates. As an insurance agent, I can pull a CLUE report for any address in America so that I can see what kind of risk I am getting the company into. You can imagine the valuable data that this provides when combined with addresses in the neighborhood. It's a fact that no insurance company on the face of the earth is going to pick up preexisting damage, for one thing. How do you think we know that? Few carriers or programs now, especially when it is a hard market, will agree to take on risk on a new property for a new owner without loss history from the seller.

But back to investors, let's consider this scenario: You and I are both purchasing occupied properties that sit right next to each other. Same neighborhood, same risks, everything. On paper they are identical risks.

But I choose to carry a $1,000 deductible, and you choose to carry a $10,000 deductible. You know by now that your insurance costs are probably going to be 20 percent less per year than mine because of that one simple variable, right?

Am I overinsured in comparison to you, then?

Not necessarily. It comes down to our goals and our financial situation. Turns out you were able to pay cash for your property, so you have the ability to dictate that deductible. I had to take a loan, so I am under the direction of my lender.

You have more skin in the game, and that's not something I can financially stomach yet. We're in a great neighborhood and in a typically moderate climate, so you may also have the ability to carve out different additional deductibles like wind/hail or theft/vandalism to save on costs.

Unfortunately you didn't obtain that all-important loss history report, so you didn't realize that our properties have both had five small water damage claims in the last seven years in the winter. It seems they aren't well insulated, which causes the pipes to freeze when temperatures get extremely low and burst as they warm back up.

I did review that report, and I knew I didn't want to deal with that loss every other year. With each water damage loss, we're both in $5,000 to get things back to whole again. After ten years there have been four more burst pipe incidents, and you are out of pocket $20,000. The $5,000 losses did not exceed your $10,000 deductible, so you had to pay for the losses in full out of pocket.

Because I knew this was a risk ahead of time, I know I am only out $4,000 (four times the $1,000 deductible) if I file a claim. But I also know that if I take steps to reduce the risk, I might be able to avoid the burst pipes entirely. I take action in the spring, before the cold snaps come, to reinsulate the house and install sensors that notify me on my smartphone when the temperature of the pipe approaches freezing. When the winter comes, the pipes stay intact, and I avoid the water damage issues altogether.

For me that higher premium for lower deductible or upfront cost to protect the property was a short-term expense for longer-term savings.

Loss Run Report

Loss run reports come in handy if you're an investor looking at a commercial property, because there are no CLUE reports for commercial properties. They are different in that they come directly from the insurance company, and they're not public knowledge. They include the same information as a CLUE, going back as long as the current owner has had the same insurance company, but you can't request them yourself. You must request that the seller provide them to you. They'll need to obtain them from their insurance company on risk.

Why would you go to all the trouble? Well, let's say you are looking at buying an apartment complex, but you want to know how much your insurance will cost before you sign the papers. This is a significant investment, and you want to know exactly what has happened in that complex in recent years. You will request the loss run report from the seller, who in turn will request it from their insurance company (through their agent) for that apartment complex.

They can't refuse, but some will try to slow walk it if there are things they'd rather hide or they don't want to lose the business. Be patient. They can't refuse the request. But this is why it is important that you don't wait until the last minute.

Okay, so you've requested the report, and when you get the report, you see that there is a pattern of repeated claims that are concerning, like arson or water damage. Even if those claims were never paid out, they stay on the record and show the date and type of loss and sometimes a brief explanation about the claim that was filed. That gives you the information that you would need to back out of a deal ahead of time.

Insurance companies do the same thing. They pull these reports and make decisions based on patterns. They shouldn't penalize the buyer for the sins of the seller, but they can get creative with your coverage packages. Even if they are fairly minor instances, if they happened frequently enough, they are going to adjust the types of losses and how much they will cover. If there have been three small fires in the last seven years, only totaling $5,000–$6,000 each, then they might decide to require a $5,000 deductible for the first year so the insurance company can pass the responsibility to the investor for future losses of similar size or severity.

And then they will say, "Let's see if you can make it profitable in twelve months and reevaluate before we entertain a lower deductible."

If the same trends continue with the new buyers that were happening with the seller, then that will be factored into the decisions moving forward.

You can sit down with your insurance agent prior to buying the complex and decide what your premiums are going to be. If I'm looking at that report as your insurance agent, and I know I'm going to be trying to negotiate the cost down for you, we are going to have to talk together about what we see.

Why This Doesn't Apply to Liability

This may be a very short section, but it's really important. Everything I said earlier is for property deductible, *not* liability. If you try to increase your liability deductible, the insurance companies are going to wonder what they are getting into with you and what kind of shenanigans you are going to try to pull behind the scenes.

DON'T NEGOTIATE YOUR DEDUCTIBLE ON YOUR LIABILITY.

Don't negotiate your deductible on your liability. I'll explain more in the next chapter, but trust me—it's not worth it.

Other Reasons to Consider a Higher Property Deductible

Let's go back to that scenario with you and me and our neighboring properties, but we're going to tweak it a little bit.

I still carry a $1,000 deductible, and you carry $10,000. This time you pulled that CLUE report and you knew what to expect. So you come up with a plan to handle it. First you save that extra money that you save on your deductible in a safe place in the event that you will need it for a water damage loss.

Second, rather than making a claim every time there is a loss, you have a local network of skilled, trustworthy contractors you know you can hire for a fraction of the cost that an insurance company would expect you to pay for the same work. You build relationships with these people so that you are ready to deploy at any time.

You end up only having one minor occurrence and can pay out that little savings you have been building up to have it taken care of without ever having to make a claim. Your premiums stay low, and you end up with more money in your pocket. In the end you have saved enough to buy two more properties on the street, and the income from those allows you to make substantial property improvements so that you never have to worry about this again. You make the entire neighborhood a more desirable place to live, thereby improving the quality of life for your tenants and neighbors.

Good for you!

CHAPTER RECAP

Insurance should be used to help manage sudden and unforeseen damage. You want to have a policy that can do that. But you certainly don't want to pay more money than you need to for this coverage. Your deductible is a part of that calculation. You want to keep your payment reasonable while providing the proper coverage for a loss you cannot or do not want to fix out of pocket. Asking the right questions of your insurance broker can help you find that sweet spot. And have a conversation with them every year to update them on the changes to your portfolio and goals. Consider factors such as your personal liquidity and the loss history on the property/properties as you choose the best deductible for your situation.

EXERCISE–CHAPTER 5

Let's say I've got a portfolio of a hundred properties, and I've got half a million dollars in the bank. There's no reason in the world I should carry a $500 deductible on my property coverage. I should look at $5,000, $10,000, or even $25,000 and save substantially on my monthly insurance premiums over time.

Now is the time for you to find that sweet spot. Go to the declarations page of every property in your portfolio and find out what the deductible is for each one. Make a list of each, and then determine if that makes the most sense for you at this time. Get in touch with your insurance agent to discuss how to make adjustments based on what you learned in this chapter.

CHAPTER 6

WHY SHOULD I HAVE LIABILITY INSURANCE?

I hope by now you're well on your way to understanding how to properly insure your real estate investment and feeling more confident about your choices.

But now it's time to brace yourself. In previous chapters I tried to keep things calm and reasonable. I offer no such promise in this chapter. In fact you're about to get the crap scared out of you. By the time you're done reading this chapter, you're going to feel the need to completely freak out and go running for your life to find your policy to ensure you

> **YOU'RE ABOUT TO GET THE CRAP SCARED OUT OF YOU.**

are carrying adequate limits of liability that allow you to sleep at night.

Okay. That was kind of an exaggeration.

But in all actuality, this is a very serious subject. Liability is the Great Unknown. There are so many options, and the stakes are very high, so this is an area where people can start freaking out a little bit—and with good reason. If something big happens, your livelihood can change and possibly the lives of others.

Whether we're talking about potential renters, tenants and their children, their guests, total strangers, or even their dogs, there is so much to consider when looking at ways to feel adequately covered. If you take this topic lightly, you risk not being fully protected, and that, my friend, can be catastrophic.

Most Important

Liability is a whole different animal in the zoo that is insurance. So far I have given you plenty of options in every aspect of property insurance, and you can see that you have the choice to carry or not carry everything I have discussed up to now. Here's where the options are taken away.

I want to be perfectly clear because I'm very, very passionate about this. Premises liability is the one type of insurance that you should never, ever, *ever* go without when investing in real estate.

To define things, premises liability is insurance for a land/property owner and covers events that occur on the real property, specifically bodily injury, and property damage to a third party caused by hazardous conditions or negligence. It is driven by the legal principle that property owners have some level of accountability for accidents and injuries on their property (or premises). It impacts businesses that own property, which includes investment properties, as they are legally responsible for the safety of invited (or even uninvited) guests to that property. Tenants fall into the category of invited guests.

Hazardous conditions that may cause bodily injury can include uneven pavement, uncleared snow, icy walks, unsecured railings, and loose deck boards, to name a few. Claims for premises liability include personal injuries that occur at the insured premises, where the property owner/investor is determined to be the negligent party. There is a property damage portion of this coverage that may also protect you if you are responsible for damaging another's property. As is true with every other type of insurance coverage, intentional acts (including criminal acts and breach of contract) are not covered.

Aside from premises liability, there are several common liability coverages that investors tend to want or need, which should not be mistaken for the *only* coverages you'll need, depending on your business. The first we commonly encounter is the need for professional liability to cover your business operations (not on an individual, per-location basis). The insured on this policy would be your business operations entity, which could be different than the entity that owns your investment properties.

This coverage can include general liability for incidents occurring at an office space that your investment business operates out of or lawsuits arising from slander or libel. This is a personal and advertising injury exposure. Some may also extend to wrongful eviction exposure (depending on the policy wording).

Side note: If you are performing renovations on a property you own and acting as the general contractor on the project, you need to obtain a general contractors liability policy with products and completed operations coverage. This extends to lawsuits surrounding faulty workmanship (not intentional) after the completion of a project. Premises liability coverage does *not* include coverage for this exposure. I want to be clear that this is a slippery slope and would require another whole book of explanation to be thorough. Because this is not a book just about liability, I encourage you to talk to the appropriate professionals and seek counsel for your specific circumstances.

Another option you can consider is umbrella or excess liability. This coverage extends the limits of your underlying premises liability in case they are exhausted on a single occurrence (and may also be able to go over other commercial liability policies such as commercial auto, general contractors, or commercial general liability). This coverage is needed when you want or are required by your lender to carry limits of liability in excess of the limits your underlying premises liability policies provide.

I take a rational but cautious approach when I meet with clients to talk about this. I want to show you why liability is the most important insurance coverage you're ever going to carry. Hopefully you never have to use it. But if ever there is a circumstance where you need it, you're going to be very happy you have it. It is your first layer of defense, and on single-family rentals and small multifamily locations, it usually isn't a huge cost for the peace of mind it provides.

Even if you're wholesaling a property and you only have ownership interest in the property for a single day, or even an hour, purchase the premises liability coverage anyway. God forbid, but if somebody were to slip and fall, get injured, or worse on that property while you have ownership interest, without liability coverage you have to pay all the damages out of pocket. And believe me when I say that can get extremely expensive.

In our program, the liability policies tend to be the most comprehensive options available on the market for residential real estate investors, because I've seen some pretty horrific things in my career that I want to do everything I can to help our investors avoid. You think your business is going great, and it may very well be. But then out of the blue you get hit with a lawsuit from an injury that happened on your property two years ago you never knew about, and you're sued for a million dollars. Liability coverages can save your business and your livelihood.

How to Know You Need Coverage Beyond Premises Liability

Commercial general liability is needed when …

- Your investment business operates out of an office and needs premises liability coverage.
- You are concerned about lawsuits arising from slander or libel lawsuits. This is a personal and advertising injury exposure. Some also extend to wrongful eviction exposure (depending on the policy wording).

Umbrella or excess liability is needed when …

- You want or are required by your lender to carry limits of liability in excess of the $1 million per occurrence and $2 million aggregate limit our underlying premises liability policies provide.

Hired/non-owned auto liability is needed when …

- You or your employees use your personal automobiles to run errands for the business. This coverage would extend if (during one of these errands) you or your employee is the cause of an accident.
- You or your employees rent automobiles for company trips and need insurance to cover them.

Errors and omissions (professional liability) coverage is needed when ...

- You offer or sell professional services (where the performance of these services could cause a loss) or could be sued for errors in judgment, breaches of duty, or negligent or wrongful acts in business conduct (*unintentional acts*).

Directors and officers coverage is needed when ...

- Directors and officers of your corporation could be held liable from the performance of their professional duties on behalf of the corporation (*unintentional acts*).

Property management professional (or property management E&O) liability coverage is needed when ...

- You are acting as a property manager. This protects all types of property management professionals if a tenant alleges that you were professionally negligent or failed to perform duties as promised in your contract.

Employment practices liability (EPLI) coverage is needed when ...

- You have employees and need liability coverage that extends to wrongful termination, discrimination, sexual harassment, and/or failure to promote.

Wrongful eviction coverage is needed when ...

- You may need protection against a problem tenant who claims to have been wrongfully evicted.

It is important to note that this coverage can be purchased as a stand-alone policy. Wrongful eviction may also be covered under the personal and advertising injury limit included on most general liability policies.

As is true with every other coverage above, intentional acts (including criminal acts and breach of contract) are not covered.

General contractors liability is needed when …

- You are licensed and acting as the general contractor on your own or your customer's renovation project.
- If you are renovating your own house yourself to sell, be sure your policy includes Products and Completed Operations. This extends to post-sale lawsuits surrounding faulty workmanship (not intentional) that was not disclosed at the point of sale.

Premises liability coverage does NOT extend to anyone hired to be on site at the insured premises who injures themselves.

Worker's compensation coverage is needed when …

- You have employees and need to provide coverage for medical benefits and wage reimbursement for employees injured during the course of employment. Employees, in return, relinquish their rights to sue you for the tort of negligence.

Cyber liability coverage is needed when …

- You are housing private information of your tenants online or collecting rent payments online.
- You need coverage for wrongful acts (an act, error, omission, negligent supervision, misstatement, or misleading statement by an insured) in connection with material on an internet site owned by the insured or related social media.

How to Do It Right

Unfortunately if you come to me and ask me how much you should carry, I can't answer that for you. No insurance agent can. There are no right answers on liability. But there are certainly wrong ones.

What you do is really up to you. I always say carry whatever limit of liability insurance it takes for you to be able to sleep at night. I know you will do everything you can to reduce risk, including installing working smoke and carbon monoxide detectors, paying for snow and ice removal, and all that other stuff. But there's no way to avoid all possible risk at all possible times in every possible scenario.

There are some pretty big numbers when it comes to premises liability insurance in order to cover you for wrongful death lawsuits and personal injuries. What I can tell you is the minimum limit you absolutely should carry, which is at least $1 million per occurrence and $2 million annual aggregate. However, please know that I am *not* saying that is a sufficient amount of coverage for your business. That's up to you to decide. Along with these insured limits, be sure that defense costs are outside of these dedicated limits of coverage per insured location. Don't ever share your primary layer of premises liability coverage among multiple investment properties you may own.

Your limits of liability reset to new limits every year at renewal. Settling for limits less than the ones I just outlined saves little to no money and jeopardizes having a sufficient amount of coverage to settle in the event of a loss. If you have a rather large portfolio of investment properties, you may want to consider higher limits of liability or an umbrella or excess policy. Remember, the more rental properties you own, the greater your liability exposure is.

If you're scratching your head at those numbers, let me break it down. It means that if a person falls through a flight of stairs that had previously been reported to you as loose, but you have not fixed it, you can be found liable for that injury. If this injured person sues you for $1 million, you are most likely covered for that. Later in the same year, if you have more problems, you're covered up to $2 million in that policy period (subject to a maximum amount of coverage of one million per occurrence). If someone breaks their ankle in a hole in the yard and sues you for negligence for $500,000, you may still be covered. But then if somebody dies (heaven forbid!) from carbon monoxide poisoning in the same year, and their family sues you for $10 million, you only have $500,000 left due to that annual aggregate limit. And wrongful death cases get expensive very quickly. Guess who is responsible for paying the remaining $9.5 million on the wrongful death loss? You.

That's a pretty extreme scenario, but you get the idea.

The good news is there are certainly steps you can take to reduce your risk. It is wise for you to clearly define in your lease who is responsible for what maintenance activities, such as snow and ice removal or lawn maintenance. This helps identify the negligent party and gives the investor something to fall back on if they are sued over something that is defined as the tenant's responsibility but should not be misconstrued as a total out.

I give every investor a list of actions they can take that can reduce the instance of liability losses, including things like logs to track battery replacements for smoke detectors, hazard checklists, and seasonal maintenance checklists. I'm not naive enough to think all my clients actually use these resources, but I'm trying to do everything I can to set them up for success if the worst happens.

These lists give you another leg to stand on if/when something happens. A fire breaks out in the kitchen, and a tenant is badly injured in the next room because they claim that the smoke detectors weren't working in the house and sues you, the landlord. You know they were working, but how do you prove to the insurance company that you had done everything you could to put protective safeguards in place that should have prevented someone from being injured if a fire breaks out?

Accurate and timely records like this help the investor remain in good standing with their insurance company. It will also help them in the long term if they want to get insured with other companies in the future. No insurance company wants to take on risk with an investor who doesn't take care of their tenants and properties.

ACCURATE AND TIMELY RECORDS HELP THE INVESTOR REMAIN IN GOOD STANDING WITH THEIR INSURANCE COMPANY.

If you lose a lawsuit like this, that record will also follow you. Remember the loss run report from the last chapter? Following a large liability loss, you may get nonrenewed, or at the very least, you will be forced to absorb a substantial increase at their annual renewal. The loss that will show up on the loss run report is permanent; however, most insurance companies only go back to five years of history when evaluating whether a property is eligible for coverage with them. So at the very least, it will negatively affect your ability to obtain cost-effective liability insurance for the next five years.

But there is also no guarantee that at five years, the loss will fall off companies' radars.

So what do you do? Well, you're going to go to your agent and ask them to find new coverage. Your agent will need to write up the narrative of what happened, and how do they make it sound good? They can't. As far as insurance companies are concerned, you're an investor who is higher-risk to them because of the lack of controls in your business.

Don't forget—frequency is as bad as severity. This is especially true with liability! If you have ten minor slip-and-fall claims over three years due to icy sidewalks, the insurance company is going to wonder why you are mismanaging the property so badly. How long before someone has a major fall and cracks their head? You are looked at as a higher risk client, and your premium will reflect that.

In these examples liability seems awfully cut and dried. But in life it rarely is. What if you have a tenant who you really like who has been a joy to have for many years? What if that person did get badly burned from a fire that happened in your house and was in the hospital for a long time? Or what if it were a baby? How would you feel?

I don't know too many investors who get emotionally attached to the properties themselves, but they certainly do with their tenants. Things get pretty complex when a tenant gets injured or passes away, and most people want to do whatever they can to make things right. I've known investors who will even pull out their checkbooks right then and there and write checks to help cover the medical bills or funeral expenses. And, as much as we can both appreciate the impulse behind this kind of gesture, it isn't the best way to handle a situation like this.

As we all know, emotions can cloud our judgment, so your insurance company will serve to keep things based on facts and not feelings. It is helpful to have an impartial third party step in and take over the claims in those instances. That way everything can be settled quickly, fairly, and as satisfactorily as possible for both sides. After all, this is part of what you pay for when you enter into an agreement with your insurance company and pay them premium.

Another advantage to having liability coverage is to help discern validity of claims. In a perfect world, there would never be a lawsuit without good reason, but we all know that isn't the case. There are websites and even books devoted to frivolous lawsuits in the United States, and the majority of them have to do with liability. Having an insurance company (and the legal defense that comes with it) on your side is an added layer of protection and expertise.

You're not the only one who has to think about this stuff. As insurance agents, we're just as much on the hook as you are when it comes to liability. What would you do if I told you that you didn't need liability coverage and you took my advice? You would very likely follow it. And then if you get sued and lose the lawsuit, you're suddenly having to pay thousands or even millions out of pocket. What do you do next? You're going to come after me, right? You're going to say I was negligent. I'm toast. I am responsible to give sound advice, to my best ability. Every insurance agent and broker should.

That doesn't mean we have to be alarmists about everything. As you know by now, we have investors who choose to self-insure their property coverage, and that's fine. Maybe they have picked up a property for $10,000 and they think, "Well, heck. If it burns down and it's sitting there vacant, who cares? Whatever. I lost $10,000. I'll clean the land up, sell it, and move on."

Depending on the situation, I may not have a problem with this.

But not when it comes to liability. Never when it comes to liability.

Are you shaking your head right now thinking I'm getting a little too extreme? I promise you all of this has and does happen in real life. You have to be ready for anything.

Things You Should Look For

I always say the way to read an insurance policy is to look at the declarations pages first. Look at the named insured, the address of the insured location, the coverage limits that you've decided upon to purchase, etc. Once you've verified that everything is correct, flip all the way to the back and look at the endorsements and exclusions because those are the ones that can really harm you. You have got to be careful about this. And don't skip over the rest of your insurance policy either; read the entire thing (no matter how bored you are).

EXCLUSIONS TO WATCH FOR

Two really common coverage exclusions on a premises liability policy are pollution (carbon monoxide) and canine (dog bites). Again, NREIG includes some coverage for both of these, but you may have to really search to find anyone else who will offer policies to adequately cover these risks. There are some that will cover canine risks, but they almost always have breed exclusions for "vicious breeds" like pit bulls and malamutes.

Let's say your tenant has a dog on your property and that dog bites someone who is walking past. Not only is the tenant going to get sued, but you will likely get named on the lawsuit as well because you own the property.

So you did nothing wrong. The tenants agreed to your requirements, signed their names promising to abide by your rules, and everything seemed fine. They started off with poodles. Cool. But now it's a year later, and they have pit bulls. It's hard to control.

If everybody listened to you as they signed the lease when you said, "Hey, no pit bulls, okay? No vicious breeds," this would be a moot point, but you and I both know that's rarely the case. You're getting dragged into the lawsuit whether you like it or not.

Side note: If you're not comfortable with the included coverage limit on your liability policy for dog bites, I suggest requiring your tenant to purchase insurance for their dog that covers these incidents. You should also require that you (or whatever your owning entity name is for the location) are listed as additional insured on their canine liability coverage. This can extend their liability coverage to you.

For pollution coverage this can be a tough one to get, but it is important to have. This provides coverage for pollutants that emanate from a heating source in your rental home. The most common issue we see is with carbon monoxide. If your tenant were to fall ill (or worse) from carbon monoxide poisoning and the leak started from a heating source inside your home, you'll be extremely happy you have this coverage. If pollution coverage is excluded from your liability insurance, you're defending and paying the damages to the injured party on your own.

DEFENSE COSTS IN/OUT

God forbid, you have a tenant pass away from carbon monoxide, and you are sued for wrongful death. Your premises liability policy is designed to provide coverage for that, right? That's why you have it. But what does that mean for the lengthy and complicated legal battle that comes with a case like this? Many times defense costs are inside that per-occurrence limit.

This is one thing that you want to be very, very careful with. If you're not insured in the right way, your per-occurrence limit of coverage could end up paying for the cost of your lawyers, and, if you know anything about lawyers, the tab adds up pretty quickly. Their services can greatly eat away at the amount of money remaining on your liability policy to pay the injured party(s) for the injuries and/or hardships sustained. With that in mind, make sure the defense costs are always outside the per-occurrence limit. This means that the per-occurrence limit goes to pay out any judgments.

Another rule is to always notify your agent of any liability occurrence that happens on the insured premises, no matter how small it may seem. We see this all the time. A tenant slips and falls and hurts his ankle. The investor landlord receives an attorney's letter informing them that the tenant slipped and fell at their property, and she has $600 worth of medical bills to deal with. The landlord starts mulling over whether to file a claim or just pay the bills out of pocket.

The landlord decides to pay the bills in an effort to settle things on their own out of court without involving insurance. The problem with this route is that when injuries are involved, there are going to be elements that aren't as clear as far as the ultimate cost. It's really hard to evaluate unless you've been in that space already. Unfortunately that landlord's decision to try to do it all alone leaves them open for the tenant to come back and hit them again when the medical bills end up being a little more than expected—or when that minor incident leads to long-term medical issues and additional substantial and unexpected out-of-pocket costs to you. And again for lost wages. And again for pain and suffering. Things just blow up in their face, and it gets to a point where they can't afford to continue to help. They decide to file a claim with their insurance company.

Now the carrier comes in and they're like, "You tried to settle on your own? Too bad. You're out of luck now."

They're not going to come in after the fact and clean up the mess, even though the landlord paid their premiums. The carrier can't help at that point. They have releases with very specific language according to state requirements, and those releases are voided when the policy-holder doesn't involve their insurance company from the start.

If the landlord pays that bill, they can still get sued, and most people can never anticipate what the defense cost will be. Defense costs include the investigation costs of the claim and everything else that needs to go into adequate representation.

The first big mistake that this landlord made was to think that it was best to keep everything from the insurance company. Your liability policy should always have what we call "MedPay" (medical payments coverage) automatically built in. MedPay typically comes with a dedicated sublimit of $1,000–$10,000 on your liability policy (depending on the insurance company's contract). This dedicated sublimit will be shown on the declarations page of your liability policy.

This means that medical payment can be paid without negligence being established so they can settle that claim, help the tenant, and put it behind you. Everybody can be happy at that point. This is why people really should consider bringing those claims to the carriers right away so they can help resolve them quickly and cleanly.

Where it gets really messy is when there are multiple people involved. Now we're looking at a situation where defense costs are going to start growing exponentially. You're looking at attorneys beating down your door, trying to figure out what's happening. You'll have all these medical expenses, and you don't know if they're legitimate or not. You have to deal with pain and suffering claims, which may or may not be legitimate. All of these things start to manifest, and if you don't have controls up front, then it can get out of hand pretty quickly.

DEDUCTIBLE/FIRST-DOLLAR COVERAGE

Premises liability policies are almost always and should be "first dollar," which means there is no deductible in the event of a claim. This is something that many people don't know. The payout on a liability claim goes to the "injured" party, whereas a property payout goes to the investor/owner. So if there is a deductible on your liability policy, you essentially have to cut a check for the deductible amount if there is a claim to cover your portion of the loss.

One investor we have in our program recently suffered from a fairly large liability loss. He called me, distraught over the fear that he was going to have to pay the $10,000 deductible that he was carrying on his property policy before insurance could help him. Imagine his relief to learn that he could turn in the claim in good conscience without any additional out-of-pocket expense because his policy was "first dollar."

HOW MANY MINOR INSTANCES ARE YOU GOING TO TRY TO COVER OUT OF POCKET BEFORE YOU DRAG YOUR INSURANCE COMPANY INTO A POTENTIAL LARGER LAWSUIT?

It should be standard, but it's a good habit to always double-check this on your policy. If you have a deductible on your liability, trying to negotiate it to be higher for a lower payment is a terrible idea because it looks like you are unable to manage your business. The carrier is going to wonder what you're trying to hide in an effort to reduce your liability premium. Remember when I mentioned earlier that frequency is just as bad as severity? How many minor instances are you going to try to cover out of pocket before you drag them into a potential larger lawsuit? Not to mention, a higher deductible doesn't really transfer into lower premiums anyway.

Single Shared Limit of Liability for Multiple Locations

You have to be very careful because, as your portfolio grows, some insurance brokers, agents, and carriers will try to save you on some premium by bundling all of your properties together as one and give you one single liability limit for your entire portfolio. You can imagine how problematic that is for investors who have large portfolios spread across many locations.

We have investors who have thousands of locations insured with us, and they buy a single $1 million for each one of their locations. I have other investor groups that buy clusters of five to ten locations, and underneath each individual LLC, they will not only buy the primary premises liability that provides the $1 million per-location, per-occurrence limit of coverage, but they will also buy a $5 million umbrella on top of that for each one of their clusters.

They do this because they had a single negative experience when working with their previous agent where they were not carrying enough liability insurance to cover a loss that happened. They were forced to pay additional funds out of pocket to make the injured party whole again. But all it takes is a tenant at some point filing a lawsuit for something that happened, and that lawsuit reaching the limits of the investor's liability or exceeding it. It might seem like overkill, but who am I to say? If they want $200 million of additional liability coverage, they should get it.

It is also a good policy to do some research into how the local government in the specific geographic location where you are investing would likely handle a lawsuit. Insurance companies do research to determine how much to charge for liability premiums. You can take an occupied single-family dwelling of twelve hundred square feet in Kansas City and pay ten dollars per month for premises liability coverage. Drop that exact property in Boston or Philadelphia, and it's forty dollars a month. This is in part because of what the carriers feel they need to make money relative to the likelihood of an event happening there. There's a larger population in Boston than Kansas City, which compounds that percentage of risk. There are also demographic and cultural trends. Parts of the country are more litigious than other parts of the country, which you can see because of history.

And there are differences in how judges tend to rule in these kinds of lawsuits. Certain cities and states tend to be more investor friendly. Some seem to want to hear both sides. And there are certain states that tend to punish the big, bad insurance company and favor the tenant.

It's similar to why you'll pay a lot more for wind/hail coverage in the Midwest than you will in the Pacific Northwest. There are certain places in the country that are more susceptible to tornadoes. You're going to be charged more in Missouri than in Idaho.

Additionally every local government interprets laws in different ways and has different expectations for property safety. One that's super common is handrails on stairs. Some places have building codes that require a handrail for three or four steps. If a property owner doesn't follow that, they are considered not to be providing a safe living environment. Other places don't specify whether a handrail is required for three or four steps.

There are so many factors that you'd do well to do a little research into your location before you determine the right amount of liability coverage for your specific situation.

General Contractor Space

Before you allow a general contractor (GC) to begin work on your property, you should require them to provide you with two proofs of insurance. The first is their certificate of liability insurance covering their business. The second (if they have employees) is their proof of worker's compensation insurance. (It's actually best to require this when they visit to bid on the job.) You should also require that your owning entity be listed as "additional insured" on their liability policy for the duration of the time they're working on site. This is usually free for them to add to their policy. This practice not only extends the contractor's liability to the investor, but it also notifies the investor if that coverage is in jeopardy of canceling for nonpayment or any other underwriting issue. The GC can't just show the document without proving they are paying for the actual coverage. It gives you the right to tell them to stay off your property until the problem is fixed.

If you have renovation property with a GC and workers on site, you really have to think about the risks present. If somebody is injured while working for you, there is always a question of who was negligent. Did the GC leave their ladder in the front yard and a person not hired to be there tripped and fell? In that situation the GC would be at fault, and in instances like that, you'll be relieved you have their proof of liability coverage on file with your entity listed as additional insured.

To be clear, injury to workers hired to be on site is not covered on any premises liability policy. And please know if you negotiate with your tenant to paint your house in return for decreased rent and your tenant gets hurt, your liability carrier could consider your tenant hired to be there. It's possible that they could decline the loss and leave you to settle it on your own. Having your tenant complete improvements at your rental home is never a good idea.

Let's say you have a property that is under renovation. The GC working on site gets stung by a hornet, so he looks around and finds the hornet's nest in the corner of the doorframe. Instead of coming back later and spraying it with a wasp spray as most reasonable folks would, he decides a better idea is to just grab a blowtorch out of his truck and burn the nest up right then and there.

You can probably guess how this scenario turns out. He'll do a great job of killing all the hornets. Unfortunately he will also do a great job of burning the house down in the process. In this scenario if this GC does not have a liability policy, guess whose shoulders it falls on to rebuild? Yup. The owner of the property—you. And guess whose rates are going up for the next five years as a result?

If the GC does have coverage, your property policy would've stepped in and paid the loss to make you whole again. They then would subrogate against the GC's liability policy to recover some or all of the funds they paid to rebuild the house.

This is a perfect example of how an insured party, through no fault of their own, will sometimes get penalized for years to come because they did not require the GC to provide them with adequate proof of insurance coverage. If the investor had done their due diligence on the GC, the story would have had a much different ending. It's these little things that can make a huge difference in the event of a claim.

Real-Life Examples

In my career I've seen some pretty horrific stuff. I'll spare you the gory details, but there are a few examples that come to mind whenever I try to explain how critical adequate liability insurance is.

I had a client who had a known drug addict as a tenant. He fell out a window and died when he was high. His family sued the owner of the property and won a full $1 million because the judge agreed the owner of the property was liable for the death since he knew the man had a drug problem and let him live in a second-floor apartment and didn't help getting him into rehab.

Another client owned an apartment complex with a sign out showing the name of the development. A tenant was driving out of the subdivision, ran a stop sign, and got into a car accident. She sued the landlord for $10 million because she claimed the sign prevented her from seeing a stop sign. She won the lawsuit. My client had a $10 million umbrella above the $1 million per occurrence included on their premises liability coverage, so thankfully he was covered.

CHAPTER RECAP

Liability could be a book in and of itself—several, in fact! The risks in this arena are seemingly endless when you consider how many things people have historically found to sue other people for. To keep yourself safe, you always want to notify your insurance agent

NOTIFY YOUR INSURANCE AGENT RIGHT AWAY IN THE EVENT OF A LIABILITY CONCERN.

right away in the event of a liability concern. Part of what you're paying for with your insurance premium is access to their defense teams. Hand it over and let them handle it. If you're turning in liability losses that turn out to be zero payout, and nothing comes out of it, it does not diminish your ability to get cost-effective, affordable liability insurance. It absolutely does not. Don't let an agent tell you otherwise. Make sure you hand it over at the onset of something potentially happening so that you don't put yourself at risk.

EXERCISE–CHAPTER 6

As mentioned in this chapter, I give every investor a list of actions they can take that can reduce the instance of liability losses. I keep a list of resources like this at nreig.com/downloadables. You can download this and other helpful tools.

Take the following checklist and fill it out for every property investment you have:

RENTAL PROPERTY HAZARD RECOGNITION CHECKLIST

OK = ACCEPTABLE / NI = NEEDS IMPROVEMENT / N/A = NOT APPLICABLE

Date: _____   Inspector: _____

RESIDENTIAL STRUCTURES

ROOF	OK	NI	N/A
Shingles in place and unbroken/uncracked			
Flashing/gutters in place, working			
Moss or overhanging trees/plant growth			
BALCONIES/DECKS			
Railing/flooring in good shape			
Items stored on railings			
Proper spacing (four inches or less) maintained between balusters			
No charcoal BBQs stored			
DOORS			
No visible damage to door or jam			
Locks in place and operational			
WINDOW/GLASS			
Glass unbroken and in good shape (including sliding doors)			
Window locks in good working order			
Security bars have inside emergency releases			
Shingles in place and unbroken/uncracked			

GROUNDS

WALKING SURFACES	OK	NI	N/A
Sidewalks/walkways are level with no major cracks			
Changes in elevation highlighted by contrast			
No standing water from rain or sprinkler overspray			
Stairway railings solid and in good repair			
LIGHTING			
All areas well lit day or night			
Bulbs all intact and in working condition			

FIRE EXTINGUISHERS			
All units mounted in plain sight; none missing			
Up-to-date annual service tag on all extinguishers			

PARKING LOTS/STRUCTURES

LOT/OPEN AREA	OK	NI	N/A
Surface free of large potholes and cracks			
No minor water damage cracks that require sealing			
Parking spaces clearly marked/painted			
Drainage working well			
No broken stops or other debris			

SYSTEMS

FIRE SYSTEMS	OK	NI	N/A
Sprinkler piping in good condition, free of leaks			
Smoke detectors intact in bedrooms, kitchen, living room, basement			
Batteries in smoke detectors still holding charge			
UTILITY SYSTEMS			
Common area electrical boxes covered and secured			
No evidence of plumbing leaks in common areas or apartments			
HVAC system filters in good shape			
Laundry dryer vents clean and unobstructed			

CHAPTER 7

WHAT THE H#!! ARE UMBRELLAS?

"Umbrella" is the most overused word in our industry.

From my perspective it seems like nobody actually knows what it means. I was on a call recently with a prospective client discussing what coverages he needed. When I brought up liability, the response I got was, "No. I don't need liability coverage. I'm going to get an umbrella, so that will cover everything."

This is the kind of comment I hear over and over again—weekly, if not daily! It's common enough that I figured umbrellas warrant an entire chapter of their own (including the closely related topics of excess liability and cyber liability), and this topic is the logical next topic after what was covered in the last chapter.

My goal isn't to make you feel bad if you don't understand what it means. The umbrella market has been in shambles in recent memory. As I write this book, it's the worst market I've ever seen. There are few people who can clearly explain what they do and even fewer who use them correctly. Even among insurance professionals, there is confusion about how to best structure property and liability insurance for rental properties, and umbrella policies can be misrepresented in this mix, which leaves landlords exposed to huge financial risks.

If you read the last chapter, you know that there's no right or wrong answer for how much liability coverage an investor should carry. That's a decision that should be made based on knowing what will help you sleep better at night. Making a decision to buy an umbrella policy falls under the same rule.

Two Options—Why They Exist and What They Do

As if there weren't enough confusion already, there is another option you'll hear about called excess liability. This can give you additional coverage and is used in a similar way to umbrellas. The two terms are frequently used interchangeably, but they are distinct from each other in a few ways.

Let's start with what umbrellas are *not*:

- They aren't magic bullets.
- They aren't catchalls.
- They don't eliminate the need for you to buy primary liability coverage (meaning you are required to hold a primary policy first).
- They do not offer any protection for your property itself. This means they don't extend to dwelling coverage, loss of rents, or anything else like that. This is hugely misunderstood, so

let me repeat. Umbrellas have nothing to do with property coverage—only with liability.

- They don't kick in until after the limits of your primary liability policy are exhausted in the event of damages or a lawsuit. Despite anything you've been told in the past, if you don't have a primary liability policy in force, an umbrella policy won't do anything for you.

With that said, let's talk about what umbrellas *are*:

- They are a way for you to garner additional liability coverage above and beyond whatever your premises or primary liability coverage already provides.
- They provide an additional layer of coverage to the owning entity listed on your liability policy as well as any additional insureds listed.

Umbrellas aren't nearly as cost effective as they were even twelve months ago. The number of carriers offering umbrella and excess liability policy options is also shrinking. It's easy to see why. It doesn't take many million-dollar payments to be made for losses that occurred for that model to fail when you're only charging $1,200 for the coverage (on average).

The lack of exclusions on some of these umbrella offerings, specifically in the hotel/resort space, has caused many carriers to leave this space altogether, even nonrenewing their umbrella policies that are profitable with no losses paid.

UMBRELLAS AREN'T MAGIC BULLETS OR CATCHALLS.

EXCESS LIABILITY

Excess liability is designed to cover losses above the limits of your primary insurance policy, and it provides an increased limit over just one specific line of coverage. In the case of a landlord, that is likely your premises liability.

DIFFERENCE BETWEEN THE TWO

An umbrella policy, while more costly, gives you more flexibility to be able to extend limits over multiple liability policies (professional liability, commercial auto liability, cyber liability, etc.). It can also extend to multiple locations, whereas excess can only put a policy over the same "type" of underlying liability policies. For example, premises liability of multiple locations cannot mix in an auto liability policy.

So, What Do I Need to Think about Before I Buy an Umbrella?

There are some general guidelines as to where I think the comfort zone is for most people I work with. Once an investor has more than ten locations in their portfolio, they probably want to look at some kind of minimal excess or umbrella policy to extend their existing liability coverage, and then they should continue to consider how that coverage should increase based on portfolio growth over time. It's a simple math equation. The more properties you pick up, the greater the risk. This doesn't mean this is the right answer for you, though. Remember, every investor, business plan, and financial situation is different. Have the conversation with your agent regarding an umbrella policy when you feel the time is right. The earlier the better.

If you look at a typical million-dollar umbrella, it's roughly $1,200 annually per million dollars of coverage, depending on where the property portfolio is located. Philadelphia, for example, could run $3,000 or more per million to cover.

The thing is it doesn't take too many shock losses to torpedo an umbrella. (If you're new to the game, when you hear the phrase "shock loss," it means a very expensive, very unexpected event. Think along the lines of a wrongful death or severe injury on one of the insured premises.)

If you have fewer than ten locations in your portfolio, I'm not saying don't get an umbrella. You certainly can, and it might be a very good option for you. But I suggest you first consider what having that umbrella policy means from all angles. When an investor gets sued, the first thing the plaintiff will do is request your insurance policy. This arms them with enough information to sue you to the limits, including any additional liability coverage you may have, such as an umbrella.

A client of mine has a portfolio with hundreds of locations. He bought a $10 million umbrella above his primary liability policy, which brought his total annual insurance payment to over $60,000. In all the time he held that policy, he had no losses, so as far as he was concerned, it was money down the drain. Was it worth it to him to have spent that much so that his conscience was at ease? Who's to say? It was the decision he made, and I agreed with him. I've seen enough shock losses to know the value of peace of mind.

This decision also depends on your history, your appetite for risk, and your anxiety level. I have some investor groups that buy five or six properties at a time and then throw a $10 million umbrella on each and every one of those on top of their premises liability. The lender(s) you're working with may also have a requirement for the limits of liability that you have to carry. This is usually determined by the maximum number of stories at any one location included on the loan. Once one or more locations has three or more stories, many lenders require, at minimum, an additional $1 million of coverage in the form of an umbrella policy. This is because the means of egress become more difficult at three or more stories. For example, if a fire breaks out on the first floor, the tenant on the fourth floor is going to have a difficult time escaping the building without injury.

I have other investors who have tens of thousands of locations insured with us with just a single, million-dollar-per-occurrence limit per location.

Neither is right. Neither is wrong. They are just different strategies. But in the end I'm never going to say no if someone wants to add an umbrella.

An umbrella is the way that you can acquire additional liability coverage up to $200 million or more if you need to. Just remember, the umbrella policy almost always "follows" the underlying liability policy, and typically anything excluded from your underlying policy is also excluded from your umbrella.

Separate Your Assets

When you are planning and structuring your business, I always recommend treating rental properties as the business that they are, which means it is more appropriate to cover them with commercial insurance policies.

Some agents who are unfamiliar with real estate investing may advise a client to insure their rental property on a personal dwelling policy (which typically includes a $300,000–$500,000 limit of liability). Then they instruct their client to purchase a personal

WHAT THE H#!! ARE UMBRELLAS?

umbrella that extends the limit of coverage over their personal home-owner's policy for their own residence as well as the investment property's dwelling policy.

Here are several reasons this may not be a good idea:

1. If you own the rental property under an entity other than your personal name (such as an LLC), the personal umbrella offers limited or no protection for that entity's asset.

2. Many personal umbrella policies contain a "business venture exclusion," which could exclude damages or lawsuits on a rental property because it produces income.

3. Most insurers only allow an individual to hold four to five dwelling policies, so if you continue to acquire investment properties, your insurer will not be able to grow with you.

4. Tying your personal assets to your business assets from a liability perspective can be harmful to you. Let's assume you have a teenager who just got their license. Two months later they make a mistake on the road that causes a serious accident, including a fatality. Your personal auto liability coverage isn't sufficient to make the victim's family whole, and you're ordered to pay additional out-of-pocket costs. Having your investment properties listed in an LLC (or other owning entity) and having them insured separately from your personal assets could prevent them from being in jeopardy following an occurrence like this.

One of our investors had a commercial liability policy with a $1 million per-occurrence limit and a commercial umbrella policy with a $3 million limit. A fire ignited at their duplexes, resulting in the unfortunate death of a tenant. The family sued this investor for negligence, and the judge awarded the family a $2.5 million judgment. The underlying commercial liability policy paid out the first $1 million, and the umbrella policy covered the remaining $1.5 million, plus extensive legal defense fees.

If that investor had not been carrying the umbrella policy, their business assets could have been responsible for the additional $1.5 million. The umbrella acted as a safety net and because it was a commercial policy not tied to their personal home and assets, their home, retirement account, savings, etc. were protected from the lawsuit.

Many investors insure their rentals similarly to the first example in the following graphic—personal dwelling policy, which typically comes with lower underlying limits of liability ($300K, for example, versus $1MM that a commercial liability policy begins at). This is why many investors feel they need umbrellas—because the underlying limits may not be enough for them to feel secure.

Personal Umbrella:

$1 Million — Extends limit of any of the below
(or a combination up to $1 mil total) if the underlying is exhausted

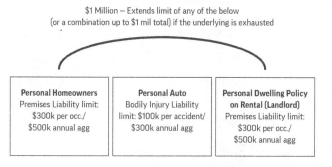

Personal Homeowners	Personal Auto	Personal Dwelling Policy on Rental (Landlord)
Premises Liability limit: $300k per occ./ $500k annual agg	Bodily Injury Liability limit: $100k per accident/ $300k annual agg	Premises Liability limit: $300k per occ./ $500k annual agg

Commercial Umbrella:

$1 Million — Extends limit of any of the below
(or a combination up to $1 mil total) if the underlying is exhausted

Commercial General Liability on Rental #1	Commercial General Liability on Rental #2	Commercial General Liability on Rental #3	Commercial Auto
Premises Liability limit: $1MM per occ./ $2MM annual agg	Premises Liability limit: $1MM per occ./ $2MM annual agg	Premises Liability limit: $1MM per occ./ $2MM annual agg	Bodily Injury Liability limit: $100k per accident/$300k annual agg

On an excess liability policy in this scenario, you can cover the 3 rentals because they are all the same "line" of coverage (premises liability), but not the Commercial Auto

Alternative:

Raise the underlying limits PER location so that you don't have to share the increased limit of an umbrella or excess with other locations or lines of coverage

Commercial General Liability on Rental #1	Commercial General Liability on Rental #2	Commercial General Liability on Rental #3
Premises Liability limit: $2MM per occ./ $5MM annual agg	Premises Liability limit: $2MM per occ./ $5MM annual agg	Premises Liability limit: $2MM per occ./ $5MM annual agg

Figure 2: *The Difference Between Personal and Commercial Umbrellas*

Designed to Confuse

Insurance companies use language that is confusing by design. It's a dirty little secret that nobody talks about. They're banking on investors (and even agents to a certain extent) not carefully reading and under-

INSURANCE COMPANIES USE LANGUAGE THAT IS CONFUSING BY DESIGN.

standing the policies, and so decisions and purchases are made based on what they *assume* rather than what actually *is*.

A popular web forum on real estate investment had a conversation about umbrellas that made me smile. If you ever feel frustrated with this concept, you're not alone. Read what one investor shared on a real estate investing forum a while ago:[5]

Can someone explain to me the difference between having an umbrella policy and having a general commercial liability policy? I need it explained like I was a 10-year-old. If I have a million-dollar General Liability policy with two million aggregate, do I even need an umbrella policy?

The response from a fellow investor was,

If somebody slips and falls on your sidewalk and sues you, your general liability policy will kick in …

An umbrella liability policy by definition provides coverage "over and above" an existing liability policy. If your costs in damages exceeded the one million limit of your general

---

5   Bigger Pockets, Forums: General Landlording & Rental Properties, accessed December 15, 2022, https://www.biggerpockets.com/forums/52/topics/941085-umbrella-policy-vs-general-commercial-liability.

liability policy, then the umbrella policy will cover whatever is above that [one million limit].

That response was pretty awesome, but it wasn't quite complete. To make sure there was no confusion, we at NREIG decided to chime in and share a few thoughts:

Umbrella policies tend to be recommended frequently to investors, but they are misunderstood and, while they work for some, are not always the best approach for everyone. Each investor situation is unique.

At the base level, there are two types of property and liability insurance policies: personal [policy] and commercial [policy]. Personal lines policies are things like homeowners (for owner-occupied properties) and personal auto. Landlord or dwelling policies are also personal lines policies.

Commercial lines policies are intended for insuring properties that are business ventures. If you own a property for the purpose of making money, even if the property is bought in your personal name, it is a business venture, and so a commercial policy is completely appropriate for this situation.

Additionally, when purchasing insurance for your investment property, you'll want to make sure you have property coverage (for physical damage to the structure) and general liability coverage (in case someone is injured on the property). For many personal lines policies, these two elements are lumped into one policy, and the liability limit is usually something like $300,000–$500,000. This means that if you, the property owner, are sued for something that happens on the *premises you own, your limit is the most your insurance will pay out in a settlement. (You will want to be sure you know if defense counsel costs are included and if they are inside or outside this limit.)*

For commercial lines policies, property and liability coverage can be bundled on one policy or two separate policies. Liability limits for commercial policies are usually higher ($1,000,000) and usually offer the ability to increase those limits.

So in your case, your DP3 policy [dwelling policy or personal lines coverage form, also called landlord policy] would cover potential damage to the property and a commercial general liability policy for injuries, etc. Typically, medical payments are part of the liability policy, not the property policy.

Because the liability limits on landlord policies are lower than commercial policies, investors often purchase an umbrella to garner additional liability protection above and beyond what that policy will pay out.

So as your fellow investor mentioned, an umbrella can only extend an underlying liability policy and only kicks in when those underlying limits are exhausted. You can extend the umbrella over multiple liability policies, as long as the named insured on the policies is the same and they are the same type of umbrella. There are personal umbrellas and commercial umbrellas, and the type of umbrella must match the type of underlying liability. You cannot put a personal umbrella over a commercial general liability (CGL) policy. And you cannot put a commercial umbrella over a personal landlord, auto, and homeowners.

We typically recommend against making any sort of connection between your personal assets (home and auto) and your business assets (rental properties). If you are sued because of an incident at your rental, it can put your personal assets at risk, and if you are sued because of an incident with your personal assets (say, a car accident), it can put your business assets at risk.

Long story short, a commercial general liability policy is completely appropriate for rental properties. It is important to work with an insurance agent who is familiar working with investment properties!

The investor then asked for additional clarification about his specific circumstance.

So, for a "commercial" policy, does the liability coverage intertwine with the landlord policy? I'm only used to landlord policies having both property damage and liability coverage. Or, is your point that a landlord policy isn't appropriate and so two separate polices are necessary, CGL and some other commercial policy for property damage? Do you see my confusion?

To which we responded,

I understand the confusion. Different insurers may structure their policies in different ways. And different agents will recommend a different insurance structure for different investors. There really is not one right way. A landlord policy that includes both property coverage and liability coverage all on one policy can be completely appropriate and sufficient. I did not mean to imply that a landlord policy is inappropriate. I just mean to say that a commercial policy (whether it is a policy that bundles property and liability or two policies: one for property coverage and one for liability coverage) is also appropriate. What's most important is being sure the agent fully explains what coverage you have (or don't have) and you are comfortable with the level and type of coverage for your peace of mind.

CHAPTER RECAP

I acknowledge that this is not a simple concept, and I know that a simple explanation like I have written here cannot possibly adequately clarify what to do in your personal circumstances.

It is important to get educated about what you currently have and what you believe you will need in the future so that you can meet your investing goals with as much coverage as you feel you require—and nothing more. As your investment business grows, it is important that you work with an insurance agent who knows the ins and outs of your specific and ever-changing needs. Look at your current policy and have a heart-to-heart with your agent about what, exactly, it is you're paying for—and what, exactly, you aren't.

Don't put your personal or business assets at risk because you feel loyal to follow some well-intentioned but detrimental advice. Commercial policies may cost a bit more up front, but they provide you coverage that is more appropriate for your business. Don't hesitate to advocate for yourself if you get any pushback from your agent. You know by now what is best for you and your business, and you can fight for it.

EXERCISE–CHAPTER 7

Consider this hypothetical scenario:

A tenant notifies you of a loose step on the staircase to the basement in their unit. For various reasons you have not yet had a chance to fix it. Now the tenant's family emails you that a family member fell through the step and tragically passed away.

Now look at the per-occurrence limit of your premises liability coverage. Are you comfortable with the amount of coverage you have in the face of a wrongful death lawsuit? If the answer is no, what amount of coverage would help you sleep at night? Call your agent and get an umbrella for that amount.

CHAPTER 8

WHAT DO YOU MEAN BY COVERAGE GAPS?

Mary invested in real estate in Corpus Christi, Texas. When Hurricane Harvey hit in 2017, one of her duplexes was damaged significantly. She called her insurance company and began the process of cleaning up as quickly as she could. The roof had been damaged so significantly that the rain from the storm came into the house. In addition the storm surges rose to a level where water entered into the structure through the doors and windows, causing more damage.

Her special form policy covered named storms, so that was good. But what she didn't realize was that it had an exclusion for floods. The first water that entered her home was rain through the damaged roof, so that was covered under the policy, but the subsequent flooding that occurred from the storm surge was not. Since it took many days for the water to abate, mold started to grow. Contractors were booked up for weeks, so nobody was available to help contain the water and damage. By the time she got anyone to come, the drywall was destroyed.

Mary was angry because she had purchased special form over basic form coverage, even though it was more expensive, because she had been told by her agent that it was "the most comprehensive" coverage she could get. She forgot that he mentioned exclusions. And now it was too late.

When Mary looked at her insurance paperwork, she got very confused about what was covered and what wasn't. Her insurance agent explained that the rule of thumb is water that comes from outside the structure is considered flooding. This is different than if her pipes had broken, which would have been water damage and would have been covered. What about if the toilets had clogged and overflowed? That would not have been covered, because sewer and drain backup are usually exclusions in special form. But her damage was considered flood, also an exclusion on her policy. The storm surge was considered a separate event to the named storm. Either way she was in thousands of dollars to clear, clean, and repair her home after Hurricane Harvey hit.

Let's say you own a structure in Florida, and you have a fire. The fire department comes in and puts the fire out. The water they use, combined with the humidity there, causes mold. That mold remediation is covered because the cause is fire. But let's say you purchased that same property and just decided to do some renovations before flipping it. You discovered the mold as you tore out the old paneling and wallpaper, and you were sad to learn that it would not be covered because mold is an exclusion.

It's the same with asbestos. If you discover it on your own, you're out of luck in terms of insurance coverage. But if you uncover asbestos because broken pipes caused the ceiling to cave in, the abatement and remediation of that asbestos are usually covered by your policy if the broken pipes event is covered.

Are your eyes crossing yet?

No need to worry. There is hope.

What Are Exclusions and Gaps?

I always say the way to read an insurance policy is to look at the declarations pages first, look at the contact information, the address of the location, the insured values that you've decided to purchase, and everything else on that page. Then flip all the way to the back and look at the endorsements and exclusions because those are the ones that can really harm you. Please thoroughly read all of your insurance policies completely.

> THE WAY TO READ AN INSURANCE POLICY IS TO LOOK AT THE DECLARATIONS PAGES FIRST

Just like you'd guess, exclusions and gaps are the terms we use for factors that are not covered by an insurance policy. "Exclusions" are perils that are not covered. "Gap" isn't necessarily an official "term" with a definition. It's just something that a property or liability policy may not cover that could be a risk. This applies to property insurance as well as liability.

When you see the term "exclusion," it doesn't necessarily mean they can never be covered (although some cannot). It just means that the policy the investor has purchased doesn't cover the peril(s) in question.

Endorsements provide clarity to coverages, coverage limits, and exclusions (where necessary) within the policy. Some even give back coverage that was earlier listed as an exclusion. For example, our program liability policy comes with a total pollution exclusion, *but* the policy is endorsed to provide coverage for pollution that emanates from a heating source, from dehumidifying equipment, or from hostile fire.

I got into the business right around when Hurricane Ike hit. This particular hurricane really changed the insurance industry and was the driver behind why we started NREIG. We saw how insurance companies in the Cincinnati, Ohio, area were handling claims at that time and figured there had to be a better way. For example, after Hurricane Ike, some carriers decided they would exclude named windstorms from property policies for locations in interior states, so they wouldn't pay "Ike-like" claims again. Others decided to get out of the space altogether. NREIG was born to provide investors with comprehensive coverage options provided by carriers that had an appetite for these risks.

The problem was that hurricanes had never caused significant damage that far inland, so Cincinnati (and other nearby major cities) were completely unprepared. The wind damage alone did millions of dollars in damage to properties that were not being charged a premium to offset a hurricane risk. This meant the number of losses that insurance companies took was catastrophic, driving premiums through the roof and opening the door for companies to begin excluding hurricane coverage on properties in Cincinnati. Hurricane Ike had an impact on the decisions by the insurance industry for a number of years. Both insurance companies and customers have had to think a little more carefully about exclusions ever since.

This chapter includes broad guidelines to help gauge your property and liability needs and determine how you might address additional risk, if desired.

Property

In the previous example, Mary discovered two exclusions in her property policy after the hurricane: flood, and mold and fungus. She didn't realize that special form coverage has a number of standard exclusions. The perils that are *not* covered on most property policies are as follows:

1. Flood
2. Government action
3. Ordinance or law
4. Nuclear hazard
5. Sewer and drain backup
6. Earth movement (including but not limited to earthquake and sinkhole)
7. Loss due to faulty zoning, poor workmanship, faulty materials, and defective maintenance
8. Wear and tear
9. Damage to property caused by insects, birds, rodents, or other animals
10. Intentional damage
11. Power failure (originating away from the described premises)
12. War (including undeclared and civil war)
13. Terrorism/political violence
14. Neglect
15. Bacteria and virus
16. Fungus, wet rot, dry rot, bacteria, and mold
17. Equipment breakdown
18. Loss of rents
19. Business personal property
20. Service lines
21. Commercial auto

On a basic form policy, everything is excluded except the causes of loss (perils) that are specifically *named* as included.

Some of these exclusions can be either purchased as endorsements to your policy or bundled as a separate policy, depending on your carrier. These perils will typically carry their own deductibles. Currently our program has options for flood, ordinance/law, earth movement, mold/fungus, service line coverage, terrorism and political violence, equipment breakdown, and a limited option for sewer and drain backup. Some exclusions such as wear and tear will never have an add-on option available. They will always be excluded because they are inevitable. Insurance companies aren't going to cover a predictable risk like having things wear out over time.

Let's get a little deeper into a few of these common exclusions and how they can put you at risk so you can begin to ponder how you might customize your property policy to suit your specific risk exposure.

EARTH MOVEMENT

Most property insurance policies contain an exclusion for earthquake (applying only to damage from an earthquake shock) or more broadly to earth movement (encompassing other forms of movement such as sinkhole).

Earthquake shock is defined as damage caused by a sudden and violent shaking of the ground resulting from movement of the earth's crust. Unlike other natural disasters, earthquakes don't have a season. They can happen at any time. They are common (more than five thousand on average occur per year in the US), and they have broad geographic risk. While earthquakes are most frequent in the states west of the Rocky Mountains, the New Madrid Fault spans many central states. While less common in the East, the older construction of many buildings in that part of the country leaves them susceptible to damage from more minor earthquakes.

Sinkhole is defined as damage caused by depressions in the surface of the ground caused by the settlement or sudden collapse of the land. Sinkholes are even tougher to anticipate than earthquakes. Where scientists are able to detect seismic activity that may pose an earthquake risk, there is no way to predetermine if there is or isn't a sinkhole on a property.

FLOOD

Regardless of the flood zone, your property is always at risk of flood. As we saw in 2022 in and around Yellowstone National Park, flooding can cause catastrophic damage to places that historically haven't been affected. Flood zones are constantly being changed/updated by FEMA, most of the time without our knowledge (unless you are one of those people who checks their website frequently). What may not be a high-hazard flood zone today could be considered one next week.

FLOOD, WATER DAMAGE, AND SEWER BACKUP ARE VERY DIFFERENT THINGS.

Also, some properties may reside in more than one flood zone. Perhaps a portion of the property sits low and has a stream in close proximity, while the rest of the property sits higher. Flood coverage is available through the government's National Flood Insurance Program (NFIP) or through private flood options. Because flood insurance policies are based on flood risk, FEMA has the final say in what flood zone you are in. Period. However, private insurers can set their rates based on factors such as age of building, elevation, etc.

You don't have to live in a designated flood zone to get insurance, but if you do, you will be required by your mortgage company to carry it. Typical homeowner's policies do not cover floods. Keep in mind that flood, water damage, and sewer backup are very different things.

TERRORISM/POLITICAL VIOLENCE

Prior to 9/11, terrorism was not typically named as an exclusion on property polices. The fallout from this event for insurers ($40 billion in property claims) led carriers to begin excluding coverage for this peril and the government to enact the Terrorism Risk Insurance Act (TRIA), which provides a federal backstop for insurers in the case of another catastrophic loss like that of the World Trade Center and Pentagon attacks.

Though intended to be temporary, it has been renewed every few years since then. It also requires that agents and insurers offer terrorism coverage to their policyholders, with the ability for the client to decline it. The coverage offered through TRIA, however, has very strict thresholds that must be met in order for any claims payouts to be made—in short, the Secretary of the Treasury must certify the event as an act of terrorism, and it must cause at least $5 million in damage. To date, TRIA has yet to pay out any claims despite mass casualty events such as the Pulse Nightclub shooting in Orlando, the Las Vegas Harvest Music Festival tragedy, and even the Boston Marathon.

In the years since 9/11, terrorist and ideologically motivated attacks have changed. In contrast to huge, well-funded foreign organizations, most acts of terrorism are lone-wolf, smaller-scale attacks. Some insurers now are offering alternative insurance options to TRIA, like NREIG, that don't have the same strict thresholds required in order for claims to be paid.

This coverage extends to losses caused by acts of terrorism or sabotage that include the use of force or violence, committed for political, religious, or ideological purposes with the intention to influence a government and/or put the public in fear. It does so without much of the bureaucratic red tape surrounding the TRIA program.

EQUIPMENT BREAKDOWN

Equipment breakdown coverage extends your property coverage to damage caused by the mechanical or electrical failure of many types of equipment at your property such as heating, cooling, refrigeration, electrical panels, and emergency generators.

LOSS OF RENTS

Loss of rents (LOR) coverage provides reimbursement to you for the rental income you would have received on a previously occupied location following a loss that renders the property uninhabitable.

If you have this coverage, based on the rental income that you would have been charging your tenant, you will be paid that money monthly for the length of time you choose to purchase coverage for, or how long it takes to make the location habitable again (whichever is shorter). If you purchased six months of coverage, but the loss takes nine months to complete repairs and get the location rented again, you're only getting six months of LOR coverage, paid monthly based on the rent amount listed in the lease. You can't collect more LOR coverage per month than what you were charging your tenant. So keep this in mind when choosing your LOR coverage limit.

Take note: Loss of rents coverage must be triggered by a property loss that is a covered peril on your property policy. You can receive reimbursement for the lost rental income while the property is uninhabitable due to the loss and therefore you are unable to charge rent.

BUSINESS PERSONAL PROPERTY

If you've partially or fully furnished your rental units (traditional rentals or seasonal), you can purchase business personal property coverage that extends your coverage to owned contents on that premises. This term is confusing, so it helps to imagine taking your property and dumping it upside down. Everything that falls out is considered business personal property. The furniture, select appliances, electronics, etc.—these items are considered property of your business. Provided theft is not excluded on the policy itself, coverage would be afforded. Most policy offerings do have a sublimit assigned to theft, especially on vacation rentals, which can help replace any items you own if they are destroyed in a covered property loss. With rentals and vacation rentals, this is a particularly important coverage to consider.

OTHER STRUCTURES

You may choose to have an included sublimit that extends coverage to detached garages, barns, or sheds that may be present at the property. If one of these structures on the property is occupied or intended to be occupied, it will need to be insured as a separate property.

SERVICE LINES

This coverage extends to repair and replacement of underground service lines (such as water, sewer, communications, electrical, etc.) that are damaged by failure of the line. Covered perils include wear and tear, corrosion, weight of equipment or vehicles, freezing, vermin, and tree or root invasion. This includes excavation costs and replacement of damaged outdoor property such as trees, shrubs, lawns, and walkways. This coverage can be added onto your property schedule or purchased as a stand-alone offering.

COMMERCIAL AUTO

If you own one or several vehicles used predominantly for your business operations, a commercial auto policy is needed to cover this exposure. Typically these policies are more cost effective than your personal auto policy because of how these vehicles are used.

Most insurance companies consider autos used for business as much lower risk. This is because, in theory, a large portion of the day, that auto should be parked at a jobsite and not out on the road. It is a very different exposure than a personal auto used for leisure.

NAMED WINDSTORM

By policy definition a named storm is defined as any storm, cyclone, typhoon, atmospheric disturbance, depression, hurricane, tropical storm, or other weather phenomenon designated by the US National Hurricane Center where a name has been applied. In our program, this coverage is included unless you request to have it removed with most property insurance options available to you. Be aware that some insurers will exclude named windstorm coverage unless you specifically request to include it. Your declarations pages of your property policy should tell you if named windstorm coverage is included or excluded, but if you are unsure, be sure to ask your agent.

ORDINANCE OR LAW COVERAGE

Many lenders are beginning to require ordinance or law coverage on residential rental properties, and you may request to have it included in your coverage package. This is often referred to as "bring-up-to-code" coverage because it offers additional reimbursement needed due to enforcement of local ordinances or laws regulating construction and repair of damaged buildings. Ordinance or law insurance provides coverage for loss caused by enforcement of ordinances or laws regulating construction and repair of damaged buildings.

Older structures that are damaged may need upgraded electrical; heating, ventilating, and air conditioning (HVAC); and plumbing units based on city codes. Many communities have a building ordinance(s) requiring that a building that has been damaged to a specified extent (typically 50 percent) must be demolished and rebuilt in accordance with current building codes rather than simply repaired.

Unendorsed, standard commercial property insurance forms do not cover the loss of the undamaged portion of the building, the cost of demolishing that undamaged portion of the building, or the increased cost of rebuilding the entire structure in accordance with current building codes.

Imagine you have a partial loss on two units of a fourplex, but the county inspection determines the building does not have hardwired smoke detectors to meet current code, which requires you to update all four units. Ordinance or law coverage can step in to help cover these updates to the undamaged portion of the building, expenses if the entire building needs to be demolished, and/or increased cost of construction if the property limit is not sufficient to meet code standards.

- Coverage A—Undamaged portion of the building: When an ordinance or law requires the insured to demolish the undamaged portion of the building following a loss, this provides coverage to that undamaged portion of the building.
- Coverage B—Demolition: When an ordinance or law requires demolition of the undamaged portion of the building, this coverage pays for that cost.
- Coverage C—Increased cost of construction: When an ordinance or law requires modifications of the building repair following a loss, this provides coverage for the increased cost of construction associated with these repairs. This extends to both the damaged and undamaged portions of the building.

LANDLORD-SPECIFIC COVERAGE GAPS

Renter's Insurance

More than 60 percent of the property losses our market experiences are "tenant-caused" negligence claims (think cooking fires, candle left burning, etc.), yet very few landlords require their tenants to carry renter's insurance. What many landlords don't realize is that underwriters look favorably on investors who enforce a renter's insurance requirement in their lease. Having this policy to fall back on following a tenant-caused loss will minimize (or eliminate altogether) your property carrier's responsibility.

A tenant came down with COVID-19 and lost his sense of smell. He lived alone in the house with his black Lab. The dog came into the house one day and was kind of acting weird, foaming at the mouth and shaking his head back and forth. The man thought something was wrong, so he took the dog down to the vet to find out.

The vet said, "Well, your dog has been sprayed by a skunk. Can't you smell it?"

He told the doctor he had COVID-19, so he couldn't smell anything. The vet sent them home with some dog shampoo, but that's about all he could do.

Eventually the man got his sense of smell back and discovered the house was uninhabitable. The odor was in the carpets, the hardwood floors, most of his clothes. Everything smelled like skunk—even his truck! He didn't know how to get it out, so he talked to his landlord. The landlord called the insurance provider, who said that none of this is covered because, even though the tenant had renter's insurance, there was an exclusion for damage by pets.

Now that's a unique scenario, but it illustrates not only the importance of carrying renter's insurance, but also knowing what exclusions are there. If you are a landlord, you should require all of your tenants to carry renter's insurance, and you need to know their exclusions.

Intentional tenant damage is always excluded from an investor's property policy because it's something that is considered uninsurable by the insurance carrier. They figure you've got security deposits that should help you through any loss, and you should have an extensive vetting policy when choosing tenants.

But if you have a situation where your tenant goes sideways with you and they start to give you trouble, you're going to have to look at other options. If you're afraid they're going to bash the walls up on the way out, there are Cash for Keys programs and alternatives to insurance that I recommend you explore.

You have to require that renter's insurance when you have them sign your contracts. You've also got to enforce that rule and make sure that you're listed as additional interest—not additional *insured* but additional interest on those renter's policies. That means you're going to be notified prior to that coverage canceling for nonpayment or any other underwriting issue. This is important because a tenant can buy a renter's policy with a month of premium up front, but if they don't pay their second or third month and that coverage lapses, investors won't know because they're not always notified.

Tenant Protector Plan (TPP)

You do your best to put language in your lease requiring all tenants carry renter's insurance and list you as "additional interest." But then you've got to make sure that the tenant's policy stays in good standing. When money's tight, the first thing that goes is their insurance policy, and you may never know.

Murphy's Law says that claims tend to happen when coverage lapses. And that's when you find out that your renters have no coverage in force.

We created our tenant protector plan (TPP) as a way to prevent our investors from being harmed by this very scenario. Our TPP coverage option allows you to offer your required renters insurance coverage as an added benefit to renting from you, instead of having to go out and buy and manage it themselves.

Many investors don't even tell their tenants they are purchasing this for them. They understand how the few extra dollars a month in premium can stabilize their property rates in the long term. They also don't want to tell their tenants they are providing them with $10,000 of

OUR TPP COVERAGE OPTION ALLOWS YOU TO OFFER YOUR REQUIRED INSURANCE COVERAGE AS AN ADDED BENEFIT TO RENTING FROM YOU.

contents coverage. That could entice the wrong type of tenant to burn their property to the ground for the $10,000 payment.

And if the tenant purchases their own renter's coverage and the TPP is also in force, now there are two layers of defense against tenant-caused negligent losses prior to the investor's property policy ultimately being left paying for the loss. The tenant's renter's policy would work as primary coverage, and the TPP coverage would provide excess coverage (if needed).

It includes a limit of liability for those tenant-caused negligent losses to pass the responsibility of the settlement to the appropriate party. It also provides contents coverage for your tenant's belongings as well as a sublimit of coverage provided for tenants of nonnegligent affected units. Additional tenants in a multifamily building are often faced with property damage from a fire or water loss in an adjoining unit. This coverage helps you lessen the burden of lost contents to those additional tenants.

Skip Rent

The last component of the Tenant Protector Plan is a unique one not easily found elsewhere. This is different from loss of rents (LOR) in that LOR has to be triggered by a property loss, where skip rent is triggered by the tenant leaving without notice—no property damage is involved. Skip rent will pay a relatively small amount ($1,000 in our case) as a one-time payment to our investor clients to cover when tenants disappear without notice. This happens sometimes. They just pack up and move without letting anyone know because they can't afford it anymore. Or maybe they die unexpectedly in the middle of the lease. Or they are deployed or evicted.

It's not a huge amount, but it can help you get over the hump before you fill that vacancy.

Many investors like the TPP because it's very aggressively priced and saves a lot of headaches in not having to worry if the renter's policy is in jeopardy of canceling for nonpayment or any other underwriting reason. With TPP you control the costs. You never have to worry about it being canceled for nonpayment.

Liability Coverage

As you learned in chapter 6, there are many different kinds of liability coverage, including premises, commercial, and general contractors. With all liability coverage, it is critical that you know what gaps exist and determine the risk you are exposed to.

POLLUTION

A majority of all personal liability policies contain a "total pollution exclusion," which is coverage for carbon monoxide. Policies developed for landlords typically provide higher premises liability limits, and some will allow you to buy back coverage to combat that exclusion. Look no further than carbon monoxide for a reason to avoid that exclusion.

Let's say you have a tenant living in your investment property who gets sick or, worse, passes away from what is determined to be carbon monoxide poisoning. Say this property is insured on your liability policy, and you have not filled this gap. You would be defending this claim on your own, which as you can imagine will get quite expensive. Avoid being left alone to defend a scenario like this by obtaining a premises liability policy that includes pollution coverage.

CANINE BITE

On homeowner's or a dwelling liability policy, the canine bite exclusion does typically exist.

On many commercial lines policies, the same exclusion applies—or at least for the fifteen or so vicious breeds (some of which you've probably never heard of). Obtaining a premises liability policy with canine bite coverage and no breed exclusions is available—you just have to find it. Unless you are dropping in on a regular basis to confirm there are no pit bulls on the premises, for instance, you could unknowingly be at risk.

ELPI/HARASSMENT

Employment practices liability insurance (EPLI) provides coverage to employers against claims made by employees alleging discrimination (based on sex, race, age, or disability, for example), wrongful termination, harassment, and other employment-related issues, such as failure to promote. It is needed when you have employees and have exposure for wrongful termination, discrimination, sexual harassment, and/or failure to promote.

TENANT DISCRIMINATION

Tenant discrimination insurance can provide property owners and managers with coverage for defense costs and loss incurred in administrative charges and lawsuits brought by current, prospective, or former tenants alleging discrimination.

ERRORS AND OMISSIONS

Errors and omissions (E&O) insurance protects companies, their workers, and individuals against claims made by clients for inadequate work or negligent actions. It is needed when you offer or sell professional services (where the performance of these services could cause a loss) or could be sued for errors in judgment, breaches of duty, or negligent or wrongful (unintentional) acts in business conduct as promised in your lease.

If you are utilizing a professional PM, you should require them to carry this coverage with you or your entity listed as additional insured. The owning entity of the property (which should be the same entity that pays the PM) should be listed as the additional insured. If you are acting as your own property manager for your rentals, you could be left exposed when acting in this capacity. These activities may include filling vacancies, setting and collecting rent, property maintenance, resolving tenant complaints, and lease enforcement. In our program, we offer a property management E&O product just for investors who self-manage their properties to fill this gap. This product also includes a sublimit for tenant discrimination.

I even purchased a professional liability policy for this book.

WRONGFUL EVICTION

Wrongful eviction coverage is needed for protection against a problem tenant who claims to have been wrongfully evicted. Important note: This coverage can be purchased on a stand-alone policy or is sometimes covered under the personal and advertising injury limit on some liability policies. It is usually reserved for liability policies offering coverage on larger multifamily locations.

DIRECTORS AND OFFICERS

Directors and officers (D&O) covers defense costs and damages (awards and settlements) arising out of wrongful act allegations and lawsuits brought against an organization's board of directors and/or officers. It is needed when the directors and officers of your corporation could be held liable from the performance of their professional duties on behalf of the corporation (unintentional acts). As always, intentional wrongdoing is not insurable. You cannot commit a crime or fraud and expect it to be covered by insurance.

PERSONAL AND ADVERTISING INJURY

Personal and advertising injury coverage entails protection from liability arising from what is said or published about an entity. Examples include slander, libel, discrimination, and, depending on the policy, wrongful eviction, etc. Very few personal and advertising injury coverages extend to wrongful eviction; it's all in how the definition is included within the policy. Your agent should be able to tell you if you need wrongful eviction and/or tenant discrimination in addition to this.

Also, many premises liability policies do not include coverage for personal and advertising injury, so obtaining wrongful eviction coverage and tenant discrimination may become necessary.

OTHER INVESTOR-RELATED POLICIES

General Contractor's Policies

Where it can be both difficult and expensive, you should only hire licensed general contractors (GC) to complete work at your property. In the unfortunate event of a loss on your property that is caused by the GC, their liability policy would be responsible for making those affected parties whole again. If you (or your entity) are also listed in a lawsuit (following the loss in question), and you are listed as additional insured on their policy, their coverage can extend to you. The minimum limit of liability insurance we recommend you require your GC to carry is $1 million.

Your premises liability policy won't extend coverage to workers hired to work at your property. As a result, hiring unlicensed handymen creates an unnecessary exposure for you and your business. If you are working with a GC who does not have coverage, your insurance company should be able to offer a policy that provides appropriate coverage.

A leased tenant you've negotiated with to paint your house for a reduction in rent falls off a ladder and injures themselves and sues you. This could be excluded for the same reason. It could be interpreted that they were hired by you to complete work at the premises.

Here are some coverages your GC should carry on their liability policy:

Products and Completed Operations

This coverage extends to the work they and their employees complete at your property. Coverage can be included for liability incurred by your contractor for damage or injuries to a third party once contracted operations have ceased or been abandoned.

Faulty Construction

Coverage on your premises liability policy is excluded for errors in construction. It is advisable that you require your contractor to carry coverage for such instances of liability. This coverage typically has to be requested to be added by endorsement to the GC's liability policy.

Worker's Compensation

Worker's compensation coverage is needed when you have employees and need to provide coverage for medical benefits and wage reimbursement for employees injured during the course of employment. Employees in return relinquish their rights to sue you for the tort of negligence.

Cyber Liability

It isn't only shock losses that can have devastating consequences. It seems like every few weeks we read stories in the news of new cyberattacks, some of which bring massive corporations to their knees. What we don't often hear about are the private individuals, including investors, who suffer because of malicious cybercrimes.

Cyberattacks are becoming more common, expensive, and devastating than ever. Data breaches, wire fraud, and ransomware are becoming almost household terms, with half of confirmed data breaches targeting small businesses, costing over $2 million on average. These costs include ransomware payments, forensic fees, notification costs, credit monitoring, and claims, not to mention legal assistance to recover.

If you collect, store, or move any information online that could potentially be used to your harm, cyber liability will probably be something that comes across your desk. This could include housing private information of your tenants or collecting rent payments online.

I USUALLY SUGGEST INVESTORS ENTERTAIN SOME LEVEL OF CYBER COVERAGE.

Keep in mind that cyber insurance is unique in the insurance industry because it's still a fairly new realm, and we are still working out the bugs. Lloyd's of London created the first cybersecurity policy in 2000. When it was first introduced, companies had no idea what they were getting into, so they came up with their best guess to charge enough premium to offset the risk. But they too often fail. Cyber criminals have done tens of millions, probably billions of dollars of damage, and people are looking to their insurance to be made whole again.

I usually suggest investors entertain some level of cyber coverage. It is well known that cybercrimes are now targeting small businesses, including real estate investors and landlords, so it is a risk that we are growing increasingly exposed to.

It is also recommended that you carry coverage for wrongful acts (an act, error, omission, negligent supervision, misstatement, or misleading statement by an insured) in connection with material on an internet site owned by the insured or related social media.

CHAPTER RECAP

Every time you get a new insurance policy, take the time to look at the declarations pages first. Double-check your contact information, address of the location, and the insured values that you've agreed to purchase to make sure no simple errors have crept in. Then after you verify that everything is correct, look at the last pages of the policy for the endorsements and exclusions. These often-overlooked parts of a policy can do a great deal of harm when you are not prepared. If you find gaps exist in your coverage that keep you from being able to have peace of mind, look into the option of adding endorsements, which can fill those holes as you gauge your property and liability needs.

EXERCISE–CHAPTER 8

Here is a checklist of the additional coverage strategies mentioned in the chapter. Cross-reference this list with your existing policies and check off what you do and don't already have. Make a plan to fill the gaps according to your goals and risk tolerance.

COVERAGE	HAVE	DO NOT HAVE	WANT TO HAVE
PROPERTY			
Earth Movement			
Flood			
Terrorism/Political Violence			
Equipment Breakdown			
Loss of Rents			
Business Personal Property			
Other Structures			
Service Lines			
Commercial Auto			
Named Windstorm			
Ordinance or Law Coverage			
LANDLORD-SPECIFIC COVERAGE GAPS			
Renter's Insurance			
Tenant Protector Plan (TPP)			
Skip Rent			

LIABILITY COVERAGE			
Pollution			
Canine Bite			
Wrongful Eviction			
ELPI/Harassment			
Tenant Discrimination			
Errors and Omissions			
Directors and Officers			
Personal & Advertising Injury			
OTHER INVESTOR-RELATED POLICIES			
General Contractor's Policies			
Worker's Compensation			
Cyber Liability			

CHAPTER 9

WHAT ELSE HAVEN'T YOU TOLD ME?

When I was around five years old, we lived with my grandparents in a home that sat on a small hill, just a little bit higher than the rest of the neighborhood. Running through the area was a creek that would flood occasionally. One year the water came particularly high and flooded every other house on the street but ours. All of our neighbors started turning in claims and were getting money from their insurance companies. But because of that hill where our house sat, we stayed dry.

I have the strangest memory of my grandma in her nightgown, leaning down and walking around the room with a spray bottle, spraying the baseboards. When she thought they looked sufficiently wet, she took pictures that she used to submit an insurance claim. Of course, as a child, I didn't understand what she was doing, and I certainly didn't care.

But now as an adult, I find this story pretty funny—and also very unfortunate, because after Grandma passed away, my mom and dad tried to sell that house. The first buyer backed out of the deal because there was a flood claim from years ago, and they were worried about that creek in the neighborhood flooding again.

Spraying your baseboards to submit a false insurance claim was fairly creative if you look at it a certain way. Illegal and unethical, yes. But I have to give her a little credit for thinking outside the box. Fortunately there are a number of much better creative investment strategies that can have more positive outcomes for real estate investors over time.

Advice for Creative Investment Strategies

This chapter will discuss several different types of real estate transactions, but the thing to *always* keep in mind for your own protection is that regardless of the type of deal, if you own the property, you insure it.

FIRST NAMED INSURED

When a property loss happens, the insurance payout check is made out to the first name that is listed on the policy. Then, hopefully, payment is made to the mortgagee and any other payee who is also listed on the policy that is appropriate.

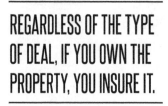
REGARDLESS OF THE TYPE OF DEAL, IF YOU OWN THE PROPERTY, YOU INSURE IT.

But mistakes happen. I have seen it time and again: investors forget to double-check who is listed first on their policy, taking for granted their agent got it right. The hard-and-fast rule is this: if you own the property, be the *first* one named on the insurance policy 100 percent of the time.

SUBJECT TO

This ties closely with first named. The term "subject to" is used when a buyer agrees to purchase a property subject to the existing mortgage, along with all other liens attached. The existing owner of the property deeds it to the buyer, who takes over making the payments from the existing lending institution rather than taking out a new loan.

We sometimes see homeowners who are in financial distress go to a "subject to" deal with a new buyer. In some cases, this means the homeowner can stay in their home and have someone else take over the mortgage payments. The homeowner can quickly get out of the financial burden of the mortgage they are no longer able to pay, while the investor has just gotten a good deal on a new investment property.

But the fact is, in an instance like this, they never notify their lender of the change. That's why it's so important that the insurance be written correctly, so the loan isn't called due.

The buyer assumes it will suffice to be added as additional insured on the seller's insurance policy and allows them to keep that coverage in force.

But what happens if the property burns to the ground? The insurance company cuts the check to the prior homeowner because that's who is first named insured on the policy, and the new owner is left with nothing but a burnt-out piece of property.

To avoid all that headache and to ensure your property policy is written correctly, if you own the property, your owning entity has to be first named insured on the insurance policy. End of story. To ensure a subject to deal is written correctly, there are four things you'll need to confirm:

1. As the owner, your owning entity should be listed as the first named insured.

2. The amount of insurance you carry has to, at the very least, be equal to the remaining amount of the loan you just assumed and meet or exceed any additional insurance lending requirements that may exist.

3. The mortgage company's mortgagee clause is listed correctly on the evidence of property insurance you purchased.

4. The mortgage company is going to require that their client's name (the seller) be listed on the coverage documents provided to them. They should only be listed on the certificate of liability insurance (explained above). Never list them on the evidence of property insurance.

COVERAGE OF NONPERFORMING NOTES

If you haven't heard the term "note" in this context before, it is just another word for loan. Often banks will go through and sell their loans off to other banks or investors. There are two types of notes: performing and nonperforming.

When a note is "performing," it means the loan is in good standing. It's being paid. "Nonperforming" notes are just what you'd expect—loans that are not being paid.

Purchasing nonperforming notes is an investment strategy that some investors prefer because they've had success in the past turning nonperforming into performing notes and have found that they may be able to charge a higher rent amount to the homeowner. It may also be they simply like the home or area and know that if they cannot turn it into a performing note, they can take the property back and have no problem renting the location out for a higher rent amount or even selling it at a higher price.

Investors who are doing this will need to buy enough property coverage to at least cover what they bought the note for, so if a loss happens, their policy will kick in and make them whole.

VACATION RENTALS

Many investors are choosing to use their investment properties as vacation rentals in lieu of having long-term tenants, especially when these properties are in desirable cities frequented by vacationers. Investors are learning they can make substantially more money renting short term. The policies designed to cover these types of investment properties are very similar to what we've been discussing throughout this book, but it wasn't always that way.

Just like Uber took the insurance industry by storm, so did vacation rental platforms like Airbnb. Insurance companies didn't quite know how to respond, so for the longest time, trying to obtain insurance coverage for an Airbnb was difficult. That's largely because the liability exposure is very different because of the frequency of tenant turnover.

The insurance industry now has some history with those kinds of properties, and they can project what their loss ratio is going to be and what they can expect to pay out on losses. We understand the security measures that are needed, such as changing locks/codes in between each tenant, using cameras, etc. Most property policies for investors don't have business personal property (or contents of a location) covered because the tenant is typically the one furnishing the rental home. Vacation rentals are fully furnished by the owner, and the coverage purchased needs to extend to these furnishings.

Other Tips and Tricks for Investors

In addition to the strategies I have listed, I have a few tips and tricks that investors can use to be more efficient and effective.

KEEP YOUR TEAM IN CONTACT WITH EACH OTHER

Investors know that it is crucial to keep your professional team of advisors in tune with one another, including your attorneys, your accountants, and your property management company. But the one person who often gets forgotten is your insurance agent.

Your insurance agent is as important as every other party in your business structure, but they are not always treated that way. In fact I know many who feel like they get treated more like a used car salesman than a professional who offers a critical service. Or they get forgotten when important business decisions are made.

> **YOUR INSURANCE AGENT IS AS IMPORTANT AS EVERY OTHER PARTY IN YOUR BUSINESS STRUCTURE.**

Let's say you decide to change your LLC name or start a new LLC and move some of your properties into that. Who is the first person you call? Chances are it's your attorney. Then maybe your property manager and accountant.

But if your insurance agent doesn't know that you've made a change and a loss happens, that new LLC has no insurable interest because it is not named on the policy. How does that claim get paid? There's a good chance it doesn't.

Let's say you have a tenant who slips and falls. They sue the new LLC because that is who they're paying their rent to, but the old LLC is still listed on the insurance policy. Guess what the insurance company can say?

"Sorry. We don't know who this LLC is. We're declining the loss."
Good luck.

By not keeping in contact, you have just given your insurance company a reason to decline the claim.

Liability is so nasty if you're not insured the right way. The first thing that the injured party's attorney will do is request your insurance policy. They'll look at the insured limits and, in most cases (if the event is serious enough), they'll sue up to the limit of coverage. If you're unable to provide them with proof of liability coverage or it's written incorrectly, you risk losing more than just your investment. They will look at your home, your vehicles, anything you own. The sky's the limit on what they could potentially get.

So my advice is to always include your insurance agent in every single important communication and decision regarding your investments. Too much information is far better than not enough in this regard.

DO YOUR DUE DILIGENCE

So you have acquired a new property, but you don't want to overinsure it. But of course you want to make sure that it's insured adequately so that you can be made whole again if a loss happens. You've decided what your risk tolerance is and what your goals are, so you know what it's going to take to recover, whether it be building a new property on that same piece of land or taking the money that you will receive from the insurance company, scrapping it, and buying something else. So you buy your policy and think that this is all the work you need to do. You consider your due diligence complete.

You need to know that the insurance company is going to do substantially more due diligence than this. They will dig in and research everything available on your property. Insurance companies are all like Big Brother; they all share information. Most of them will actually agree to take on risk without having the full scope of the picture. But they give themselves thirty to sixty days to come back after they do their additional due diligence to make sure that they have all the information. This also provides them with adequate time to complete an on-site inspection to assist with uncovering any hazards that may exist that they were previously unaware of. If there are on-site hazards they find during the inspection, you'll be given usually thirty to sixty days to comply with their requirements to fix these hazards, or your coverage will be canceled. Our hazard checklist walks you through what these inspectors are looking for when they visit your property. We are giving you the answers to your test before you have to take it.

They could find out if there was arson that may have occurred or a history of repeated vandalism in the area, and they can adjust their rates accordingly after you have your policy in place. Then they will come back and say, "You didn't let us know that there had been three different fire claims in the span of twelve months. We agreed to a $500 annual premium for your insurance, but now we're going to need to charge you $2,700 due to the added exposure."

Or they'll simply cancel your policy altogether because they no longer feel the risk with your property is an acceptable one. And then you're stuck because many insurance companies share data in an effort to keep the industry as profitable as possible. You won't be able to shop around and get a cheaper rate at that point.

If you're buying from a homeowner, get that comprehensive loss underwriting exchange (CLUE) report. If you're buying from another investor, get that loss run report from their current insurance company. Do your research. Know what you're buying.

MEET OR EXCEED INSURANCE LENDING REQUIREMENTS

It's important that you meet or exceed the insurance requirements of your lender the first time through. Seasoned real estate investors don't worry as much about this because they are usually working on this early and often. But if you're newer to the game, always get a list of the insurance requirements from your lender and give them to your insurance agent as early as possible in the process.

When I meet with a new client, I make it a practice to give them a set of coverages based on my understanding of what they want. I always tell them that I can't guarantee that my list will match that of their specific lender. However, providing me with your lender's insurance lending requirements will allow me to guarantee that the coverages I recommend to you meet or exceed their guidelines the first time through.

If you neglect to do this, it can (and often will) delay your closing, because the lender won't fund the project without assurance that you have met their requirements. This is one of the most common reasons that closings are delayed. Having adequate coverage ready to be put in force at the time of closing is crucial to your deal funding on time.

All you have to do is request the set of insurance lending requirements from your lender when you meet with them. Any competent insurance agent or broker will know how to structure their coverage to meet or exceed every requirement on that list.

WARNING SIGNS

There are a few things that you can (and should!) watch out for when shopping for new insurance. This list is not comprehensive, of course. Rather it contains a few of the biggies that I have noticed through the years.

INFLEXIBILITY

There will never be flexibility with how claims are settled, unfortunately. Where there is flexibility is on the insurance-to-value requirements among carriers. Some carriers understand the advantages of allowing an investor to insure a location to a lower valuation per square foot and don't solely look at the few dollars in premium they aren't collecting in doing so.

Others only look at it one way, which is not advantageous for investors. It's never only about how much premium they are collecting. Think about a twelve-hundred-square-foot home in Nashville, Tennessee. Carrier A allows its investor client to insure the property on replacement cost for $108,000 (or $90 per square foot). The annual property premium is $540. Carrier B requires that same investor to insure the same property for $210,000 (or $175 per square foot). The annual property premium is $1,050.

Now let's assume that property burns to the ground. Does the additional $567 that Carrier B collected offset the additional $102,000 they would pay in this total loss scenario?

Not even close.

And the kicker is this professional investor is probably more than okay with insuring the property to $108,000, because it's either adequate for the amount of money they have into it, or they are confident they can rebuild it for $108,000.

Flexibility and options are key when you are shopping insurance carriers, as is partnering with an agent who understands this.

Questions You Should Ask Your Broker

I tell everybody, even my own clients, that every couple of years you should be shopping proactively with other agents. I figure if you can go to another agent who will do a better job than me, I deserve to lose your business. So regardless of the personal relationship, I should be doing the best I can for you. Insurance is a roller coaster. The market changes about every twenty-

> **YOU NEED TO BE PROACTIVE AND SHOP YOUR INVESTMENT INSURANCE JUST LIKE YOU DO FOR HOME AND AUTO.**

four to forty-eight months. It hardens and it softens. There are ups and downs. You need to be proactive and shop your investment insurance just like you do for home and auto.

Now when you're shopping for a good agent or broker, one of the first questions you should ask is what carriers they represent. Then find out if they're involved in real estate themselves. That's a huge advantage because they'll understand your needs.

Find out if they are familiar with your specific market by asking if they are representing investors in the area that you're looking to purchase a property. Obviously the Memphis market is different than the San Diego market, right? You want an insurance agent who understands your market and can give you the right kind of advice and guidance. It helps if they are active in real estate investor associations.

Here is a short list of basic questions you can consider asking when you're shopping around:

1. How many insurance companies that are comfortable insuring investment properties are you contracted with?
2. Do you have errors and omissions insurance? What limit do you carry? (If they don't have insurance, run!)

3. In what state(s) are you licensed to sell property and casualty insurance? (They have to be licensed in the state where your rental property is located to advise on and sell you insurance.)

4. Have you worked with my lender on previous loans?

5. Who will be my main point of contact in your office after I initiate coverage?

6. Whom do I submit claims to if one happens? How do I reach them?

7. Are all of the insurance companies you are with A rated or better by A.M. Best?

8. Can you provide three current client references I can contact? Ask for other investors with portfolio sizes similar to yours, in similar areas of the country.

9. Who are your main competitors, and how are you superior to them?

10. Are you an investor yourself? Do you belong to or do you sponsor any local real estate investor groups or associations? Which ones?

11. What does my renewal process look like with your agency? How many insurance carriers will you shop my coverage out with each year? How far in advance of my renewal will I receive my upcoming annual terms?

When you go armed with these questions and anything else that you have learned in this book, you can make decisions that are the most appropriate for your circumstances. I encourage you to be brave enough to say "no, thank you" to anyone who is pushing an agenda that does not match your goals. You are a valuable client, and your business is an asset, not a liability, to any company you choose to work with. You don't have to settle for anything less than what you know you need.

CHAPTER RECAP

As you have probably guessed by now, there are more considerations when it comes to real estate investment insurance than I could possibly cover in one book. Every investor is unique. Every property is also. The best book would be one that was written just for you and updated as often as your needs changed. But since that's impossible, I leave you with these parting thoughts: assess your risks, do your due diligence, and keep clear on your goals. Insurance should grant you peace of mind, not give you headaches.

FINALLY, RIGHT?

If you couldn't tell by now, I love getting in with investors when they're starting off. As they succeed, we succeed with them.

I want to challenge you to ask questions of your insurance agent. They are the experts on this matter, sure. But don't be afraid to say, "Hey, I have some concerns here, and I just want to make sure that I have this covered right."

Do your homework on a property before you invest in it or decide to acquire it. There is all kinds of information out there readily available for you to do that. Take a look at all the data, and find out what the quality of a property is before you buy it. Know what potential issues you can expect to see that are controllable. Know what your rental income projections are, what your flood and earthquake exposures are. Maybe there are losses in the past that you weren't made aware of that could harm your ability to obtain cost-effective insurance.

> **TREAT YOUR INVESTMENT PROPERTIES LIKE THE BUSINESSES THEY ARE.**

Partner with the experts who can actually give you that data to make sure that it's a property you want to invest in.

NREIG was founded to help investors like you. You might be doing this as a side job or a weekend hobby. You could be working on a flip to make some side cash. Most know pretty quickly if this is for them or not. For those who love it, they just continue to grow their portfolio. Usually when they get to around ten to fifteen cash-flowing properties on their rental portfolio, they can become a "full-time investor."

At that point it's getting out of the grind of the nine to five. It's about freedom. It's about time. It's certainly about a passion for investing in real estate.

You've got a million things on your plate. Acquiring property insurance is the last thing on your mind, but insurance is the thing that most often puts roadblocks on deals.

As a final recap, here is a quick list that I always share to help investors make the best decisions.

1. **Treat your investment properties like the businesses they are.**

   Combining personal and commercial policies can jeopardize everything. If your policies are structured the proper way and a large loss occurs, you can be made whole again after a loss, and your policy will work in the way that insurance is supposed to work.

2. **Shop your rates.**

   I suggest working with an independent agent who is contracted with several carriers and programs. They should be able to offer the widest range of options. Be careful that you don't simply choose the cheapest plan without carefully reviewing the details. You could be risking the coverage that you need just to save a few dollars.

And don't wait until your renewal is a few days out and you are blindsided with a large increase in premium with no time to shop. Your agent should be proactively shopping your portfolio sixty to ninety days out from your annual renewal. If that isn't the case, I recommend shopping yourself—for a new agent.

3. **Pick the best form for you.**

If you are comfortable self-insuring some perils and taking on the added risk of potentially paying out of pocket for certain perils, consider transitioning from special form to basic form. This can save you 20 percent or more per year. There are additional exclusions on the basic form that you need to watch, so read your declarations page carefully and confirm with your lender they are okay with you moving to basic form prior to doing it. Jeopardizing coverage to save money is never a good idea.

4. **Consider carrying a higher property deductible.**

This can offset some or all of the increase in premiums. Simply put, the higher the property deductible you carry, the lower the property rate they assign. (But be careful not to overextend yourself!) Increasing your property deductible from $1,000 to $5,000 could save you as much as 25 percent.

5. **Leverage your portfolio size.**

If you own multiple properties, consider combining them all into a single master policy. This will almost always drive your premiums down.

6. **Improve security and fire safety.**

   Some carriers will provide credit for proof of working hardwired smoke detectors, central station burglar alarms, and sprinkler systems. Give your agent as much ammunition as you can to prove you are doing your due diligence to reduce the risk. Even if the carrier insuring your properties cannot provide credits, these are best practices that all investors should consider.

7. **Use a hazard checklist.**

   Having sound risk management procedures to present to an insurance company underwriter is a powerful rate-decreasing tool. See our sample hazard checklist at the end of chapter 6.

8. **Require and enforce renter's insurance.**

   Many rental property owners have a clause in their lease requiring tenants to carry this. It's a good idea for them and a bonus for you because it will save you money in the long run. Let's face it, a tenant is more likely to do something negligent like leaving a faucet running, a curling iron plugged in, or a candle burning than you are. Having a renter's insurance policy in force allows tenant-covered loss to be paid for by their insurance company rather than yours.

9. **Don't give the insurance carrier a reason to deny a claim.**

   If you are reviewing your declarations page on your policy currently and are unsure if you have the correct type of policy to cover your non-owner-occupied dwelling, email your agent and ask them for clarification. We always recommend you use email, so you have their response in writing. If something happens in the future, you will have leverage in the event of a declined claim, if needed.

10. **Know what you have.**

   Take the time to get educated about what you need and compare it to what you have. Be particularly aware of exclusions and gaps and don't hesitate to ask your agent for more if you think you need it.

My goal in writing this book was to make it easy and to make sure that I have educated my readers on the points that you need. If your insurance is not structured correctly, those slip-and-falls and other unknowns that occur at the property can destroy you—not only by jeopardizing your business, but in your personal life too. You think your business is going great when suddenly you get hit with a lawsuit from something that happened at a property owned for as long as it took you to drink a cup of coffee.

Insurance language is designed to confuse, and it's our job to make it easy for our clients so that they understand what they're getting into in terms of exclusions, endorsements, and language within a policy that can harm them.

But now that you are armed with the most current information out there, you can cut through all the noise of the insurance industry and make the very best decision for your goals and your portfolio.

WHAT MAKES NREIG SPECIAL?

National Real Estate Insurance Group (NREIG) has been in business since 2008 and is the largest and longest-running insurance program in the country for residential real estate investors.

We figured out that the one-to-four-family residential real estate investing insurance market is very underserved, and we've developed a program that meets the needs for the residential real estate investor.

We work with investors on how to make sure that insurance isn't a burden for them. We try to make it as easy and as seamless as possible for our clients to be able to rest at night knowing that their properties are insured, and then not to have to worry about it too much during the day.

Our goal is to be a one-stop shop for everything an investor needs. That's kind of the secret sauce for our company because we sell property and liability coverage as well as ancillary coverages that are important to our investors, whether they want them, need them, or are required to have them by their lender. We offer coverage options for investors across the country with products that no other company offers. I think it's safe to say that we know what we're doing.

Here's why we are different:

- We offer unique coverage and benefits that cater to our clients' specific needs and business models—no "off-the-shelf" policies.
- We use a monthly reporting form with no minimum earned premium.
- We waive coinsurance for anything over $60/square foot.
- We offer replacement coverage at $80/square foot.
- We cover occupied, vacant, new construction, and renovation properties.
- We are continually adapting and expanding.

Customized Policies

We offer customized coverage options because we know that not all investment strategies are the same. And we know that means your insurance strategy will not be the same as other investors.

We don't tell you what type of insurance you need to purchase. Instead of us just sending you a quote, like you're accustomed to getting from your agent, with us you actually get assigned a sales advisor who takes some time to ask you questions like, "What's your appetite for risk? What's your exit strategy? Is there a lender on the deal?"

Then after getting to know your specific circumstances, we give you a list of your options, with the information about each option, and then allow you to pick the option that best fits your needs.

Investors should always have choices when it comes to insurance. It's not one size fits all.

Side note: As with all retail agents, we do not have the ability to adjudicate claims, which means NREIG is not the one paying claims after losses. Rather, we work as an advocate on behalf of our clients and our insurance carrier partners to come up with the best fit for both parties ahead of time, and we work hard to keep the process running as smoothly as possible throughout.

Flexible Master Policies

One of the advantages to the program is that for an investor who has a hundred locations, ninety-eight of those will typically run smoothly. But when two of them have a bad year (like multiple arsons or two or three theft claims), our program has the ability to just isolate those two locations and negotiate with the carrier where they may want more money for those two locations because of the losses that happen.

This means the investor doesn't experience an increase in the other properties. Most other insurance providers will either cancel the entire policy, all hundred locations, because of the mistakes of two properties, or they're going to pass that increase along for the entire portfolio.

Monthly Reporting Form

A monthly reporting form is what allows our clients to make changes to their coverage and pay for only what they need each month, with no set minimum earned premiums or long-term commitments. Our clients receive monthly invoices reflecting their current inventory, which we encourage them to review and report any changes on an ongoing basis. These changes include newly acquired properties, sold properties, insured property value, or occupancy status, to name a few. Whether you have a single-unit property or a hundred multiunit apartment buildings with up to twenty units per location, we offer a single form so you can track your policies for your entire portfolio and seamlessly transition services as needed.

With other companies, if you are going to renovate a property, you must purchase a six-month or twelve-month policy and pay it in full at the onset of coverage. When the renovations are done within three months, and you need to flip that over to an occupied policy, you find out that you were subject to a minimum or fully earned premium percentage. These diminish or eliminate any return premium you would've otherwise been due for the unused time left on your policy.

We take that guesswork out of the equation.

We offer a self-serve, online portal as well as more than seventy licensed agents who take calls over the phone. So it's as simple as letting us know that the location changed from occupied to vacant or vice versa, and all we do is just flip the switch in our system, and coverage continues as normal. This eliminates the need to cancel policies, start new ones, and wait for returned premiums that could create cash-flow issues.

Coverage without Coinsurance

We offer coverage without coinsurance, provided you ensure your property to at least $60 a square foot. Coinsurance can be kind of a dirty word in insurance because it can diminish the amount of money that you are able to recover following a loss. We don't like it, so we don't have it on our program offerings to our insureds. And we'll do everything in our power to keep it that way for as long as we are here.

We offer replacement cost coverage beginning at $80 a square foot, which is substantially lower than what most insurance carriers and providers offer. Typically you're required to insure to $90–$120 per square foot (at minimum) to get replacement cost coverage.

Some insurance agencies will tell you how much coverage you need to insure a property for. We let our investors tell *us* how much they need to insure their property for, within reason. We know that we have savvy investors out there who are our clients, and they know how much it will cost to rebuild in their area. That's why we allow them to pick their coverage limits.

> WE LET OUR INVESTORS TELL *US* HOW MUCH THEY NEED TO INSURE THEIR PROPERTY FOR.

Occupancy Status Flexibility

We have the flexibility to accommodate every type of occupancy status collectively on one schedule, including vacant, occupied, and renovation properties. If you are starting to play in the multifamily space or are currently investing in it, we can accommodate for those larger-unit-count locations across the country.

We cover ground-up construction. We cover vacant properties, whether they are boarded up and secured to sell or with renovation planned in the future. We can insure vacation rentals within our program. We cover mobile and modular homes and some light mixed-use retail inside our program. We even cover nonperforming notes on our lender-placed alternative insurance.

All of this is an effort to eliminate the need for you to have to buy individual policies for each and every one of your properties. We are trying to respond very quickly and be out ahead of the curve to make sure that our investor clients never have to go anywhere else for any coverage. And we'll continue to evolve according to the state of the property market.

Adapting and Expanding

My team is always working very hard to plug any gaps or holes we potentially have to make sure that our clients are covered. Here's a list of a few of the specialized offerings that we have developed in recent years:

- Tenant discrimination
- General contractor liability (for flippers who find it very difficult to get that coverage)
- Canine liability with no breed exclusions
- Terrorism and political violence
- Equipment breakdown
- Property management errors and omissions
- Tenant protector plan
- Renter's insurance (sold directly to tenants)
- Service line
- Earth movement
- Private and NFIP flood

We also have a full lines commercial agency for any risk that doesn't fit in our program, and we have niche programs such as StorageGuard, CannGuard, GCGuard, InkShopGuard, and Inker by InkShopGuard.

If you are interested in discussing how NREIG can help you insure your portfolio, go to NREIG.com, or call (888) 741-8454.

WHAT EVERY BROKER SHOULD KNOW (AND SAY)

I get kind of blunt when it comes to talking to my peers and colleagues in the business. If you don't do things the right way—you're not educating clients, you're trying to just give them the best deal, and it's all price driven—you're never going to get anywhere. You're going to chase your tail constantly.

Tip 1: Stop cutting corners.

This is my most important piece of advice for everyone in the insurance business. Stop sending one proposal out and just waiting for the email to come back saying, "I want it" or "I don't." Stop acting like every coverage is exactly the same for every investor—and that there aren't choices for them to choose from.

You need to be extremely thorough so you can adequately educate your clients. I know it's a little bit more work on the front end, but you're going to reap the rewards on the back end because then those people don't leave you.

Nobody makes money while they're building their book of business. Just like so many other businesses, you make your money on your renewals. Take the necessary time to build a relationship, get to know your client, and clearly explain the options they have available to them. As your investor client grows, you grow. They will bring additional properties to you without hesitation because they trust you.

I tell my clients that they should be shopping for new insurance every couple of years just to make sure they are keeping me on my toes and I'm giving them the best coverages and the best price. If I'm not, they should fire me. I recommend you do the same.

Of course, a lot of them don't do that because they trust us because of the amount of time we put in with them, but I don't ever want to take anything for granted.

Tip 2: Document everything.

Put *everything* in emails. I know it's a pain to sit and type recaps of every single phone call, but it's worth the time. And it doesn't have to take too much time. Come up with a template that you can use that goes something like this:

> *Dear [their name],*
>
> *Per our conversation at ___ time on ___ date, we discussed _____.*
>
> *The decision(s) made was/were _____. I will be taking the following action: _____.*
>
> *If anything is incorrect, let me know right away. If not, your silence will be taken as agreement.*

Thank you for your business,

[Your name]

Be sure to have a read receipt set up to come for all of your important emails so that you have a record that the client at least opened the email. This comes in handy if they contact you with quick questions on coverages. But it also is crucial to help mitigate mistakes. In our case, we've got twenty-two thousand investor clients with seventy people on calls with those investors. Mistakes are going to happen.

DOCUMENT EVERYTHING.

In a worst-case scenario, you could be defending your position in court because of a discrepancy or misunderstanding on what was discussed and agreed upon. You have evidence with this record of emails that can help to provide clarification.

Tip 3: Give it the time it needs.

Patience is definitely an important element of being able to make sure that your clients understand what you're telling them. If you don't spend time with them or educate them in the beginning, you're going to spend that time later, and it's not going to be as comfortable a conversation.

Tip 4: Stay educated.

Training and education for the agents and brokers are so important. I emphasize current training with my team so that we can put constant, valuable information out to our investors. That's the name of the game because if you don't educate and empower them, they'll find an agent who will.

Tip 5: Build your online presence.

Along the same lines, be aware of your online presence and what is happening online in our industry. It's no secret that there are a few agents who do slimy stuff. They'll increase premiums 30 percent with no explanation. They'll hold the renewals to the last minute, so their clients don't have time to shop. It happens a lot. But what they underestimate is that when these investors search the term "investor insurance" or "landlord insurance," NREIG pops up. I need ten minutes, and I can provide the terms they want.

GLOSSARY

This glossary is not exhaustive of every specific term we use in the industry but rather covers some of the most commonly used words and phrases.

Actual Cash Value (ACV) Coverage: In the event of a covered loss, claims are settled with a deduction for nonrecoverable depreciation and the selected deductible.

Additional Insured: A party who is afforded coverage under the premises liability coverage but isn't notified if coverage is in effect and isn't a claim payment recipient.

Agreed Value Policy: An insurance contract for which the value is agreed upon in advance and is not related to the amount of the insured loss.

Aggregate Limit: A contract provision used in insurance to limit the amount that can be paid in the policy period. An aggregate limit is the maximum dollar amount your insurer will pay to settle your claims.

Apartment: A residential structure with five or more units in one building. Typically these have a common entrance and hallway.

Basic Form: Less comprehensive coverage than special form. Covered causes of loss must be specifically named in the policy.

Builder's Risk: Insurance that covers a building where the building or insured area is presently being constructed. Another name for renovation properties.

Claim: An insurance claim is a formal request to an insurance company for coverage or compensation for a covered loss or policy event.

Coinsurance: A property insurance provision that states the amount of coverage that must be maintained as a percentage of the total value of the property for the insured to collect the full amount of a loss. Common coinsurance values are 80, 90, or 100 percent of the value of the insured property.

Commercial/Mixed-Use Structure: Nonresidential dwelling or property that does not meet the criteria of other property types. Includes but is not limited to mixed use, retail, office buildings, warehouses, hotels, etc.

Condominium: A collection of individual home units and common areas along with the land upon which they sit.

Deductible: A specified amount of money that the insured is responsible for before an insurance company will pay a claim. This amount is taken from claims settlements before the payout is sent to the client.

Depreciation: A reduction in the value of an asset with the passage of time. This is calculated at the time of loss based upon the age, condition, and useful life expectancy of the damaged property.

Flood: Defined as (A) a general and temporary condition of partial or complete inundation of two or more acres of normally dry land area or of two or more properties (at least one of which is the insured property) from 1. overflow of inland or tidal waters; 2. unusual and rapid accumulation or runoff of surface waters from any source; 3. mudflow; or 4. rising water or an intrusion due to heavy rains; or (B) collapse or subsidence of land along the shore of a lake or similar body of water as a result of erosion or undermining caused by waves or currents of water exceeding the cyclical levels that result in a flood.

Insurance to Value: The relationship between the amount of insurance purchased and the amount required to rebuild your home.

Invested Capital: Actual purchase price, less land value, plus verifiable cost of improvements completed at time of loss.

Loss Payee: A party that isn't notified of coverage being in effect but would be the beneficiary of claim payments.

Loss of Rents: Coverage is only for a covered loss that renders the home uninhabitable and that requires your tenant to be temporarily displaced while repairs are being completed at the home. (Please note that this coverage is limited to the necessary time needed to repair the home and bring it back to a habitable condition, not to exceed twelve months.)

Loss Ratio: The percentage of incurred losses to earned premiums.

Manufactured Home: Factory built, frame construction, delivered via truck, and prepared on site.

Medical Payments: A general liability coverage that reimburses others, without regard to the insured's liability, or medical or funeral expenses incurred by such persons as a result of bodily injury (BI) or death sustained by accident under the conditions specified in the policy. This coverage does not extend to tenants. This would effectively address how medical payments are viewed.

Medical Payments (Tenants): Tenants and/or those who regularly reside at the residence premises are typically unable to recover payment under the medical payment provision of the liability coverage. This means that coverage extended to tenants and/or those who regularly reside at the residence premises is generally addressed through the $1MM or $2MM policy limits offered and the insured in most every circumstance has to have some measure of negligence contributing to the loss or event before payment can be considered. Excluded causes of loss will not be paid regardless of negligence.

Minimum Earned Premium: The smallest amount of money an insurance company is willing to accept in exchange for a policy.

Mobile Home: A dwelling that at one point had wheels (must not currently have wheels and must be on a permanent foundation).

Modular Home: A dwelling that never had wheels and is similar to mobile home construction.

Mortgagee: The party that has made the loan on the property. Generally they are a payee on the claim payment because of their interest in the property. They receive information in regard to coverage being in effect.

Multifamily Dwelling: A two-to-four-unit residential dwelling that is on a single lot or parcel of land under the same ownership.

Named Windstorm: By policy definition, a named storm is defined as any storm, cyclone, typhoon, atmospheric disturbance, depression, hurricane, tropical storm, or other weather phenomenon designated by the US National Hurricane Center and where a name has been applied.

Negligence: Failure to exercise reasonable consideration resulting in loss or damage to oneself or others.

Nonperforming Note: A nonperforming loan (NPL) is the sum of borrowed money upon which the debtor has not made their scheduled payments for at least ninety days. A nonperforming loan is either in default or close to being in default.

Occupancy Status: Classifies all dwellings according to whether they are occupied, vacant, or under renovation during the time period of the data collection. In our program, we use the client's intent for the property within sixty days to determine the occupancy status.

Owner Occupied: Owners occupying the described property.

Per-Location Deductible: If a client has a per-location deductible, a deductible will be applied to each location in the event of a loss.

Per-Occurrence Deductible: If a client has a per-occurrence deductible, the deductible would only be applied once if more than one home is damaged in the same event.

Peril: An event that causes damage to property or injury; a cause of loss.

Replacement Cost Coverage: Allows claims to be settled with reimbursable depreciation.

Shock Loss: An unexpected and significant enough loss that does enough damage to a property as to cause financial distress.

Single-Family Dwelling: Single, free-standing residential dwelling that typically includes a yard. The structure normally sits on a single lot or parcel of land. Townhomes are conjoined units that are owned by individual tenants. They are similar in architecture to rowhomes in that the owners share at least one wall. These are both single-family units as long as there is not an HOA in place. Manufactured homes are also single-family homes. These are factory built, frame construction, and delivered via truck and prepared on site.

Skip Rent: When a tenant does not pay the rent that is owed for a property.

Special Form: More comprehensive than basic form; inclusive of all sudden and accidental perils except for those that are specifically excluded in the policy.

Subrogation: A situation where an insurer, on behalf of the insured, has a legal right to bring a liability suit against a third party who caused losses to the insured. The insurer maintains the right to seek reimbursement for losses incurred by the insurer at the fault of a third party.

Sublimit: A limitation in an insurance policy on the amount of coverage that is available to cover a specified type of loss.

Theft: The unlawful removal of property.

Townhome: A multistory house in a modern housing development that is attached to one or more similar houses by shared walls. Typically the client is responsible for the interior and exterior of the structure.

Umbrella and Excess: Coverage for liability above a specific amount set forth in a basic policy issued by the primary insurer; or a self-insurer for losses over a stated amount; or an insured or self-insurer for known or unknown gaps in basic coverages or self-insured retentions.

Underwriter: A person or service that evaluates and assumes the risk of another person or group for a fee.

Valued Policy Law: State legislation that specifies that the insured shall receive the face amount of the policy in the event of a total loss to a dwelling rather than the actual cash value regardless of the principle of indemnity.

Vandalism and Malicious Mischief: The destruction or damage of property without theft.

Water Damage: Sudden and accidental damage to property done by water. Insurance does not cover damage resulting from an insured's negligence or failure to maintain home repairs.